THE KOKINSHŪ

TRANSLATIONS FROM THE ASIAN CLASSICS

THE KOKINSHŪ

Selected Poems

Translated and Introduced by

TORQUIL DUTHIE

Columbia University Press

New York

Columbia University Press wishes to express its appreciation for assistance given by the Pushkin Fund in the publication of this book.

Columbia University Press
Publishers Since 1893
New York   Chichester, West Sussex
cup.columbia.edu

Library of Congress Cataloging-in-Publication Data
Names: Duthie, Torquil, translator, writer of added commentary.
Title: The kokinshū : selected poems / translated and introduced by
Torquil Duthie.
Other titles: Kokin wakashū. English
Description: New York : Columbia University Press, [2023] |
Series: Translations from the Asian classics |
Includes bibliographical references and index.
Identifiers: LCCN 2022028948 (print) | LCCN 2022028949 (ebook) |
ISBN 9780231207621 (hardback) |
ISBN 9780231207638 (trade paperback) |
ISBN 9780231557054 (ebook)
Subjects: LCSH: Waka—Translations into English. |
Japanese poetry—Heian period, 794–1185—Translations into
English. | Kokin wakashū. | Waka—History and criticism. |
Japanese poetry—Heian period, 794–1185—History and criticism. |
LCGFT: Tanka. | Literary criticism.
Classification: LCC PL758.22 .A3 2023 (print) | LCC PL758.22
(ebook) | DDC 895.61/108—dc23/eng/20221206
LC record available at https://lccn.loc.gov/2022028948
LC ebook record available at https://lccn.loc.gov/2022028949

Cover image: Gen'ei Manuscript of the *Kokinshū*.
Tokyo National Museum

For Angela and Niall

CONTENTS

CONTENTS

ACKNOWLEDGMENTS

LIKE MOST southern Spanish cities, Cádiz has many plazas. They are all kinds of shapes and sizes, each with their own mood, and all connected by the maze of winding streets. There are majestic ones like San Antonio, and magical ones like Plaza de Mina. But there are also smaller, less remarkable ones that bring fond memories, like the Plaza de San Agustín. Originally home to an Augustinian convent in the mid-seventeenth century, the convent cloisters were transformed in 1863 into the city's first public institute of secondary education. That was where I went to high school, during the night shift, from 6:45 to 10:30 pm, with a lively and good-humored group of mostly nontraditional students.

I must have been sixteen when my Spanish literature teacher assigned a presentation on the poetry of Antonio Machado (1875–1939). I liked poetry but wasn't a big fan of Machado. Perhaps it would be fairer to say that I didn't think much of the poems I had encountered: some stuff about the sea, which I thought was okay, but also about faith and finding one's path, which I found unrelatable and tedious. My copresenters (we were a team of four) must have thought so too, since they had stuck me with the subtopic "Machado and Religion."

Feeling somewhat at a loss, I asked my father for advice. My father has always preferred reading novels to poems, but he sat down, took a look at the book, and after a while handed me a piece of paper with several lines of scrawled fountain pen ink. Among several suggestions, I saw he had written, *Machado trata de retarse y de rezar* (Machado is trying to challenge himself and to pray). I found myself raising my eyebrows in surprise at the pairing of *reto y rezo* (challenge and prayer)—my father's native language is not Spanish and he is not a religious person—and then protested: "I can't use that, it's too good—the teacher will realize it's not me." My father grinned and said, "No, he won't—you should use it."

So I was shameless and I did. The teacher didn't say much at all—just nodded encouragingly throughout. I don't remember anything about my presentation except those two words. I do remember one of my copresenters whispering to me on the way back to our seats, "hey, you had some good stuff there!" And I remember other things about that day: the names and nicknames of my copresenters (whom I have not seen since that school year), the order in which we were sitting (I was second from the right), and the order in which we spoke. Why all of this detail? I think it is because the memorable pair of words that my father gave me have somehow highlighted the memory. *Reto y rezo* have stuck in my mind since then, gently nudging me over the years to look for patterns in words and be a more curious reader.

■ ■ ■

Like most Scottish cities, Edinburgh has many hills. Most famously Castle Rock and Arthur's Seat, but also between them to the north is Calton Hill, where David Hume is buried, and where my parents rented a flat shortly after moving from Cádiz, some fifteen years after my presentation on Machado. It was there, while I was visiting from New York over Christmas and Hogmanay of the year 2000, that my mother gave me an English translation of Machado's poems by the Scottish poet Don Patterson. I opened it with some anticipation (I have never been given a bad book by either of my parents) but also a bit of apprehension (I had never read an English translation of twentieth-century Spanish poetry that I liked). Patterson's book did not adopt the usual parallel version format with Spanish originals—his versions had the entire page to themselves. What surprised me most of all was the *tone* of the translations— so different from the Machado I remembered, and yet they worked so well. This Machado was a lot more playful than I remembered—or perhaps it was that Machado *could be read* as being playful? Perhaps the problem that sixteen-year-old me had with Machado was not that Machado was too serious and a bit boring, but that I was? As I read the translations, I found myself trying to recollect and recreate Machado's originals. Then sometime later I bought a Spanish edition, and proceeded to rediscover Machado as a poet that I remain very fond of to this day. That was my mother's real gift to me—the delight of transposing words from one linguistic world to another and the magic of moving back and forth between languages.

■ ■ ■

I had planned to complete this book before our daughter was born. She is now five. Her name rhymes with brave (and with wave) and her smile rhymes with her mother's.

■ ■ ■

I am grateful to all the students who have taken and enriched my seminars on the *Kokinshū*. Thanks to Christopher Sturgis, who proofread the manuscript. To David Lurie and Haruo Shirane—thank you for your kind encouragement. Special thanks go to my editor, Christine Dunbar, for her deft handling of the entire publication process, and to Christian Winting, Kat Jorge, Ben Kolstad, and Maureen O'Driscoll. I am also grateful to the anonymous readers for Columbia University Press, for their numerous comments and observations that have greatly improved the book.

Finally, I want to acknowledge the great intellectual debt I owe to Lewis Cook. Were it not for his graduate seminar on *Kokinshū* commentaries in Spring 2001, this book would probably never have been written. Readers familiar with Lewis's scholarship on Sōgi will also recognize the influence of Sōgi's ideal that the poems of the *Kokinshū* should be "read beautifully" (*yūgen ni yominasu beshi*), as texts that do not have one single conclusive interpretation.

THE KOKINSHŪ

INTRODUCTION

THE *KOKINWAKASHŪ*, or *Collection of Ancient and Modern Japanese Songs*, more commonly known as the *Kokinshū*, is an anthology of some eleven hundred poems compiled in the early tenth century at the Heian court. The "Japanese songs" (*waka*) of the title are a vernacular poetic form of thirty-one syllables divided into five measures in a 5/7/5/7/7 pattern. The emphasis on "Japanese" (*wa*) marks an explicit contrast with the cosmopolitan style of Sinitic poetry, which was also popular among Heian aristocrats. The collection (*shū*) is "ancient and modern" (*kokin*) because it anthologizes poetry written by its editors and their contemporaries together with poems from both the recent and distant past.

The *Kokinshū* was compiled to create normative models for waka composition and to bring waka poetry to the forefront of the cultural life of the court. To say that it succeeded in this aim would be an understatement. From shortly after its completion to the end of the nineteenth century, the *Kokinshū* was revered as *the* classical text that served as the cornerstone not only for the composition of waka but also for later forms of vernacular poetry, such as linked verse and haikai, and for the tradition of vernacular literary writing that developed from poetry collections and commentary. The status of the *Kokinshū* at the Heian court is evident from its extraordinary number of citations in the vernacular prose writings of the period. The famous anecdote in Sei Shōnagon's *Pillow Book* about an empress memorizing the *Kokinshū* in its entirety may be hyperbolic, but it cannot be too far from the truth given that the *Tale of Genji* contains more than two hundred fifty allusions to the anthology. Its enduring position as the foundational collection of the waka tradition is attested by the more than three hundred commentaries on the *Kokinshū* produced from the twelfth to the twentieth centuries. This vast commentarial tradition led to many of its poems becoming the source material for all kinds of other literary forms, including the Nō theater and late-medieval popular fiction. In sum, the *Kokinshū* is a fundamental point of entry for readers interested in premodern Japanese vernacular literature.

This book is a translation into English of roughly one-third of the anthology—343 poems out of 1,100—and its two prefaces. In part due to their brevity, waka do not convey meaning as self-contained artifacts, but rather do so in dialogue with other poems written on similar topics. How one understands any single waka poem will depend greatly on the degree of one's familiarity with other poems. Moreover, the *Kokinshū* is an anthology that encourages readers to interpret its poems in relation to each other. It deliberately organizes them into sequences of themes, so that poems echo earlier poems or fore-shadow later ones, in many cases complicating and adding layers to what readers thought they had understood. The objective of this book is to translate the poetic language of the *Kokinshū* as a whole, in such a way that English-language readers can understand and experience how its poems work together to create a literary world.

I have written this book so that it may be enjoyed by specialists and nonspecialists alike and have endeavored to make the translation accessible to people who cannot read Japanese, classical or modern. For this reason, unlike most translations of waka, which tend to be accompanied by Roman alphabet transcriptions of the original Japanese text, the poems are presented only in English translation. I want the translations to stand alone, without having to lean on the authority of an original text that may be inaccessible to the reader. That being said, nothing would make me happier than if this book were to inspire people to study classical Japanese and read the original *Kokinshū* in a Japanese modern scholarly edition, or perhaps even to learn cursive script and read it in manuscript form. Readers who can read an original text also know where to find one, that is, if they do not already possess one.

The translation is accompanied by eight essays on various aspects of the *Kokinshū*. The essays are an important part of the book, but it is not necessary to read them before the translation. In fact, I would encourage first-time readers of the *Kokinshū*, in particular, to begin with the translation, and then read the essays either in the order they are written or at different times and in any sequence you wish.

PART I

TRANSLATION

MANA PREFACE

WAKA TAKE ROOT in the ground of the mind and open their blossoms in the forest of words. Inasmuch as people exist within the world, they cannot possibly remain unmoved: Their thoughts and cares easily shift; their sorrows and joys constantly change. Emotions grow forth from sentiments, and their reciting takes the form of speech. This is why the voices of those at ease are full of joy, while the cries of those in distress are full of sorrow.[1] Waka make it possible to express one's concerns and reveal one's frustrations. There is nothing more suited than waka to move heaven and earth, affect demons and spirits, transform human conduct, and harmonize husband and wife.

---

[1] This opening section draws on two famous passages from the Chinese classics: the "Mao Preface" to the *Classic of Poetry* and the "Music" chapter of the *Record of Rites.*

There are six principles of waka. The first is called Suasion; the second is called Exposition; the third is called Comparison; the fourth is called Evocation; the fifth is called Elegance; the sixth is called Panegyric.[2]

The spring warblers chirp amid the blossoms, and the autumn cicadas cry above the trees. Though they do so with little variation, they each display their own songs. This is an inherent principle of all living things. During the Seven Reigns of the Age of the Gods,[3] times were simple, and people were forthright, there was little distinction between emotion and desire, and there was still no waka composition. The first recitation of thirty-one letters occurred when the god Susa-no-o arrived in the Land of Izumo.[4] This was the origin of what is now called an envoy. After that, everyone used waka to communicate their feelings, even the grandson of the Heavenly Gods and the daughter of the Sea Deity.[5]

[2]   These six principles are identical to those in the Mao Preface to the *Classic of Poetry*. Even in their original context, it is unclear what each of the principles signifies, but the point of listing them is to advance the claim that waka is an elevated form of literary expression equal to the tradition of Sinitic poetry.

[3]   The mythical age of the gods, as described in the first two volumes of the earliest imperial history, the *Nihon shoki* (*Chronicles of Japan*, 720 CE), and other texts, such as the *Kojiki* (*Records of Ancient Matters*, 712 CE).

[4]   This is the first example in the *Nihon shoki* of a waka poem in five measures and thirty-one graphs (kana graphs representing syllables): "Rising eight clouds / Izumo eightfold fences / to keep my wife / eightfold fences I build / ah yes those eightfold fences."

[5]   This refers to a poetic exchange in the *Nihon shoki* between Hiko hoho-demi (son of Ninigi) and Toyotama-hime, the daughter of the Sea God, from whose union the first emperor Jinmu was born.

When the reigns of human sovereigns arrived, there arose many styles, such as Long Songs, Short Songs, Head-Turnings, and Mixed-Bases.[6] The various forms were of many types and developed profusely, just like the trees that touch the clouds start as a tiny breath, or like the waves that soar into the sky begin as a drop of dew.

Now, when it comes to the Naniwazu verse presented to the Heavenly Sovereign,[7] or the Tomi River piece in response to the Crown Prince,[8] these are either related to miraculous affairs, or involved in mysterious matters.[9] But if we examine the songs of high antiquity, most of them had ancient and simple diction, did not yet indulge in playfulness of the ear or the eye, and served

6   The usual distinction between "long songs" (*chōka*) and "short songs" (*tanka*) is that tanka refer to the common five-measure thirty-one syllable form, and chōka to longer compositions. "Head turning" refers to *sedōka* poems, an archaic form of six measures in a 5/7/7/5/7/7 pattern of which the *Kokinshū* includes only four examples. The term "mixed-bases" (*konpon* 混本) is a mystery.

7   Naniwazu was the palace of the legendary Emperor Nintoku (313–399 CE). The "Naniwazu verse" is cited in the kana preface. The poem also appears on *mokkan*, wooden slips used for writing practice, from archaeological sites going back two hundred years before the compilation of the *Kokinshū*.

8   A reference to a poem that appears in *Nihon ryōiki* (1:4), as the response from beyond the grave of a dead beggar whom Prince Shōtoku had identified as an immortal sage: "The Tomi Stream / running through Ikaruga / were it to cease / only then would the name/ of our lord be forgotten." The poem is also included in the *Shūiwakashū* (*SIS* 20:1351).

9   Nintoku and Prince Shōtoku each represent the two pillars of cultural knowledge commonly referred to as the "Outer Writings and Inner Classics" (*gesho naiten* 外書内典). The "Outer Writings" are the Sinitic classics, which according to legend, arrived in Japan during the reign of Nintoku's father Ōjin, when Nintoku was crown prince. The "Inner Classics" are the Buddhist teachings, whose introduction to Japan is strongly associated with the figure of Prince Shōtoku. Through this rhetorical pairing, waka is portrayed as participating in all forms of cultural knowledge.

only for moral instruction.[10] In ancient times, on beautiful days in fine seasons, the Sons of Heaven would command their ministers attending banquet to present waka. It was then that the lord could observe the feelings of his subjects and thereby distinguish the characters of the wise from the foolish. And by such means they were able to follow the people's wishes and select talented officials.

From the time that Prince Ōtsu first composed odes and rhapsodies,[11] literary men and talented masters yearned for those styles and followed in their tracks. When the letters of that House of Han[12] were transmitted, our sun-region's customs[13] were transformed; the endeavors of the people were entirely changed, and waka gradually declined. However, there was an old master, the court official Kakinomoto,[14] who above all displayed the most marvelous sentiments and from ancient to modern times stands alone without peer. There was also Yamabe no Akahito.[15] These two are the sages of waka. Furthermore,

---

[10]   The idea that poetry should serve for moral instruction derives from the Mao Preface, but in fact, very little suggests this was the case in early Japan in the poems collected in the *Kojiki* and *Nihon shoki*, or in the *Man'yōshū* (*Collection of Myriad Ages*, ca. late eighth century).

[11]   That is, Sinitic poetry. Prince Ōtsu was a son of Emperor Tenmu. According to the *Nihon shoki*, "the composition of odes and rhapsodies started with Ōtsu."

[12]   Refers to Sinitic writing.

[13]   Refers to the realm of Japan.

[14]   Kakinomoto no Hitomaro was active during the late seventh and early eighth century and has been widely recognized as the greatest poet of the *Man'yōshū* since at least the early Heian period and probably since the time of the compilation of the *Man'yōshū* itself.

[15]   Akahito was active in the second quarter of the eighth century. He is an important poet in the *Man'yōshū*, but the notion that he was equal or a close second to Hitomaro is not one that early modern and modern commentators shared with their Heian and medieval predecessors.

for a long time, there came many others who made waka their endeavor. But then the times turned shallow, and people began to admire sensuality. Frivolous words arose like clouds, and currents of charm bubbled up like hot springs. All the fruit was fallen, and only the blossoms were in bloom. In the houses of the amorous, waka were treated as flowery and flighty go-betweens, and even beggarly monks used them to make a living. And thus it was that they became mostly a method to entertain womenfolk, and inappropriate to present before court officials.

In recent reigns there are, moreover, barely six people who maintain the old styles.[16] And yet each of them have their own strong and weak points, so it is necessary to discuss these in order to distinguish them. The Hanayama Bishop's songs achieve an excellent style, but their diction is flowery and lacks fruit; they are like a painting of a beautiful woman who moves people's feelings in vain. The Ariwara Captain's songs are full of feeling, but their diction is lacking; they are like a wilted flower

---

[16] These six poets later become known as "the six sages of waka." They were all active during the second and third quarters of the ninth century. Three of them are well-known figures and prolific poets: "the Hanayama Bishop" is Yoshimine no Munesada (816–890), a grandson of Emperor Kanmu (r. 781–806), more commonly known as Archbishop Henjō and the author of seventeen poems in the *Kokinshū*. "The Ariwara Captain" is Ariwara no Narihira (825–880), a grandson of Emperor Heizei (r. 806–809), who is the author of thirty poems in the *Kokinshū*. Ono no Komachi (fl. mid-ninth century) is the author of eighteen poems in the *Kokinshū* and the subject of many later legends and Nō plays. The other three poets are more obscure: "Bunrin" is the Sinified name of Fun'ya no Yasuhide (fl. mid-ninth century), who is the author of five poems in the *Kokinshū*. Priest Kisen (dates unknown) is the author of a single poem in the *Kokinshū*, and Ōtomo no Kuronushi (dates unknown) is the author of only three poems in the *Kokinshū*.

with little color remaining that still has fragrance. Bunrin composes skillfully, but his style is a little vulgar, like a merchant wearing a beautiful robe. As for Priest Kisen from Mount Uji, his diction is too ostentatious, and the beginnings and endings of his songs are inconsistent; they are like watching the autumn moon when suddenly at dawn it is covered by the clouds. Ono no Komachi's songs are of the same school as Princess Sotōri[17] of ancient times; they have charm but no vitality, like a sick woman wearing makeup. Ōtomo no Kuronushi's songs follow those of Sarumaru Daifu[18] of ancient times; they are rather splendid, but their style is terribly uncouth, like a peasant who stops to rest by some flowers.

In addition to these, we know of countless other names, but most of them take charm as the basis of their craft and know nothing of the true import of song. As for the majority of people, they are interested only in glory and profit and have no use for reciting waka. What a truly sad state of affairs! Even if one were to rise in position to become both a minister and a general and one's wealth were to increase to a vast sum, this would

[17] According to the *Nihon shoki*, Princess Sotōri was a concubine of the legendary Emperor Ingyō (traditional reign dates, 412–453 CE). The comparison with Komachi is probably due to a poem attributed to Princess Sotōri in *Nihon shoki*: "This is the night / that my lover will come / thus it is shown / distinctly in the patterns / of the spider's web," which suggests the figure of a woman waiting, as do many of Komachi's poems (e.g., see *Kokinshū* 656 and 1030; hereafter cited as *KKS*).

[18] Sarumaru no Daifu is an obscure legendary poet who may never have existed. In medieval texts, he is credited with numerous poems that in most cases are demonstrably apocryphal. The anonymous *KKS* 215 (translated in this book) is attributed to him in the *Ogura hyakunin isshū* (*One Hundred Poems by One Hundred Poets*).

still not prevent one's bones from rotting in the earth and one's name from becoming extinct in later ages. It is only those who practice waka who are known to later times.[19] This is because their words are close to the ears of the people, and their sense accords with the understanding of the gods.[20]

Long ago the Heizei Son of Heaven commanded his officials to compile the *Collection of Myriad Ages*.[21] From then until now ten reigns have passed, and more than one hundred years have elapsed. During that time, waka was abandoned and no collections were made.[22] Even if there were some who possessed the airy elegance of Minister Ono, or the lighthearted touch of

[19] This recalls a famous line in Cao Pi's (187–226 CE) "Discussion on Literature" (*Lunwen*): "The years of our lives have their time and are then extinguished. Glory and pleasure come to an end with one's mortal body: as they both inevitably reach their normal span they cannot compare to the immortality of literature."

[20] This line is open to various interpretations, but in my reading, "close to the ears of the people" emphasizes the character of waka as *vernacular* poetry (as opposed to the cosmopolitan register of Sinitic poetry), while "their sense accords with the understanding of the gods" points to the relationship of waka with the mythology of the imperial lineage.

[21] The *Man'yōshū* was compiled throughout the eighth century over a period of at least eighty years. At the time of the *Kokinshū*, little was known about the circumstances of the compilation of the *Man'yōshū*. Emperor Heizei reigned from 806 to 809. The sense here may be "the Heijō Son of Heaven," which could refer to any of the sovereigns who reigned from the Heijō Palace throughout the eighth century ("Heijō" and "Heizei" are different readings of the same graphs). Similar to the Kana Preface's mention of "the reign of Nara," it is probably intended to be deliberately ambiguous.

[22] There were no collections of waka, but three collections of Sinitic-style poetry were imperially commissioned during the reigns of Saga (r. 809–823) and Junna (r. 823–833) at the beginning of the ninth century: the *Ryōunshū* (814), the *Bunka shūreishū* (818), and the *Keikokushū* (827).

Counselor Ariwara,[23] they are all known for other talents, and it was not this path that brought them to fame.

Prostrate we submit that since His Majesty has ruled the realm it has been nine years. His humaneness flows beyond the Dragonfly Islands and his compassion is as abundant as the shade of Mount Tsukuba. The voices that complain of pools becoming shallows are all silent and everywhere are heard wishes that grains of sand become rocks.[24] Thinking to renew the airs that had since ceased and desiring to reestablish the path that had long been abandoned, His Majesty commanded Senior Inner Secretary Ki no Tomonori; Director of the Palace Library Ki no Tsurayuki; former Junior Clerk of Kai Province, Ōshikōchi no Mitsune; and Assistant to the Right Palace Guard, Mibu no Tadamine,[25] to each present song collections from various houses and old songs from ancient times. This was called the *Collection of Myriad Ages Continued* (*Shoku Man'yōshū*). Then we were further commanded to classify the songs we had collected and compile them into twenty volumes.

---

[23] Ono no Takamura (802–852) is the author of six poems in the *Kokinshū*, of which three (*KKS* 335, 407, and 961) are translated in this book. Ariwara no Yukihira (818–893) is the author of four poems in the anthology, of which two (*KKS* 23 and 962) are translated here. It is significant that both of these figures composed poems in exile (*KKS* 961 by Takamura and *KKS* 962 by Yukihira), which may be read as an allegorical allusion to the marginal status of waka in their time.

[24] Meaning that there is no criticism and only praise of his reign.

[25] These are the four compilers of the *Kokinshū*. Tomonori's dates are unknown, but he appears to have died before the compilation of the *Kokinshū* was completed (see *KKS* 839); Tsurayuki (872?–945) was the main compiler of the *Kokinshū*. Mitsune's dates are unknown but he is thought to have died around 925. Tadamine's dates are also unknown but he is thought to have been born around 850.

This was then named the *Collection of Ancient and Modern Japanese Songs* (*Kokinwakashū*).

As for us subjects, our words have little of the charm of spring blossoms, and our reputations are stolen from the long autumn nights. Though we proceed in fear of the ridicule of the times and retreat in shame of our clumsy talents, we feel fortunate to have lived during the revival of waka and rejoice at the renewed prosperity of our way.

Ah! Hitomaro may be gone but are waka not here with us?[26] In these times of the fifth year of Engi, a junior-wood ox year,[27] in the fourth month on the eighteenth day, Tsurayuki and the others[28] humbly present this preface.

---

[26] An allusion to *Analects* (9.5): "King Wen may be gone, but is *wen* (culture) not here with us?"

[27] The year 905 (according to the Gregorian calendar) was the fifth year of the Engi era (during which Emperor Daigo reigned) and a junior-wood ox year according to the cyclical sexagenarian calendar.

[28] The authorship of the Mana Preface is attributed to Ki no Yoshimochi in *Honchō Monzui* and in extant manuscripts. But this closing makes it clear that the preface is written in Tsurayuki's voice.

SELECTED POEMS FROM *KOKINWAKASHŪ*

VOLUME 1—SPRING SONGS 1

Composed on a day when the first day of spring arrived within the old year

Ariwara no Motokata

1   Spring has arrived
        before the year's end:
   the present year,
        Should we call it "last year"?
        Or should we say, "this year"?[1]

---

[1]   The Heian court used a combination of lunar and solar calendars. According to the solar calendar, the first day of the year began on the first day of spring (which corresponds to February 4 in the Gregorian calendar). But the New Year in the lunar calendar began on the day of the second new moon after the winter solstice, which could fall sometime between two weeks before and ten days after the solar new year. This meant that once every two or three years the first day of spring (of the solar calendar) preceded the lunar calendar's last day of the year. Some commentators interpret the compiler's choice to begin with a poem about the coincidence of the new with the old as an allusion to the "Ancient and Modern" in the anthology's title.

Composed on the first day of spring

Ki no Tsurayuki

2 That water where
  I drank and drenched my sleeves
before it froze,
  today that spring has come
  will it melt in the wind?

Topic unknown

Author unknown

3 Where could it be
  that the spring haze is rising?
In Yoshino,
  the fair hills of Yoshino,
  snow continues to fall

A royal song on the beginning of spring by the Nijō Empress Consort[2]

4   Spring has arrived
                before the snow has gone;
       perhaps now
                the warbler's frozen tears
                will melt away at last?

Topic unknown

                              Author unknown

5   Though the warbler
                that has come to the branches
       of the plum tree
                cries to summon the spring,
                snow continues to fall

---

[2]   Fujiwara no Takaiko (842–910). Daughter of Fujiwara no Nagara and sister
       to Chancellor Fujiwara no Mototsune (836–891), she was empress consort to
       Emperor Seiwa (850–878, r. 858–876) and mother to Emperor Yōzei (869–949,
       r. 876–884).

Composed on snow falling and covering the trees

Dharma Master Sosei

6   Perhaps he thinks
            they are blossoms because
        spring has arrived?
            White snow covers the branches
            on which the warbler cries

Topic unknown

Author unknown

7   So profoundly
            have my thoughts been suffused
        by my desires,
            that the lingering snow
            appears to me like blossoms

According to some, this is a song by the former Great Minister of the Realm.[3]

---

[3]   Fujiwara no Yoshifusa (804–872), grandfather of Emperor Seiwa.

When the Nijō Empress Consort was known as the Bedchamber Lady Mother of the Spring Prince,[4] *on the third day of the New Year he was summoned, and as she conveyed her commands, at her request he composed on the snow that had fallen on his head even as the sun was shining*

Fun'ya no Yasuhide

8   Though I may be

     graced by the shining rays

   of the spring sun

    I am vexed by the snow

    that lies atop my head

Composed on falling snow

Ki no Tsurayuki

9   The haze rises,

     and on budding trees spring

    snow is falling,

     so even blossomless gardens

     are now covered in blossoms

---

4 The Nijō Empress was Fujiwara no Takaiko. The title "Bedchamber Lady" (*miyasundokoro* 御息所) referred broadly to consorts of the emperor. "Spring Prince" refers to the crown prince. The headnote is noting that the poem was composed after she gave birth to the crown prince but before he became emperor (Yōzei), that is, between 869 and 876.

Composed at the beginning of spring

Fujiwara no Kotonao

10   Is spring early

      or are the blossoms late?

    The warbler's voice

      that would resolve this question

      is nowhere to be heard

A song at the beginning of spring

Mibu no Tadamine

11   People may say

      that spring has now arrived

    but I think not,

      for as long as the warbler

      has still not come to sing

Songs from the Empress's Song Contest in the Kanpyō Era[5]

Minamoto no Masazumi

12   In the crevices

    of the ice that is melting

in the valley wind,

    are those waves that emerge

    the first blossoms of spring?

Ki no Tomonori

13   The blossom's scent

    I entrust to the messenger

that is the wind

    and send it as a sign

    for the warbler to visit

[5] This headnote refers to poems 12–15. The Kanpyō era was from 889 to 897, during the reign of Emperor Uda (866–931, r. 887–897), one or two decades before the compilation of the *Kokinshū*. The contest took place in 893, at the residence of Uda's mother, Emperor Kōkō's empress consort, Hanshi (also called Nagako, 833–900).

Ōe no Chisato

14   Without the voice
    of the warbler emerging
from the valley,
    who could possibly tell
    that the spring has arrived?

Ariwara no Muneyana

15   Spring may have come,
    but where no blossoms flower
in the mountains
    it is with a sad voice
    that the warbler is singing

When the Ninna Emperor[6] was still a prince, he sent someone spring herbs with this royal song

21   It was for you
            I set out on spring fields
        to pick young herbs,
            as the snow kept on falling
            on the sleeves of my robe

Composed and presented when he was commanded[7] to present a song

Tsurayuki

22   Is it to pick
            the young herbs in the fields
        of Kasuga,
            that the people are walking
            as they wave their white sleeves?

6   Emperor Kōkō (830–887, r. 884–887).
7   By Emperor Daigo (885–930, r. 897–930).

Topic unknown

Ariwara no Yukihira no Ason

23 The robe of haze
   in which the spring is dressed
  has a thin weft,
   and could easily unravel
   in the mountain wind

Composed at the Empress's Song Contest in the Kanpyō Era

Minamoto no Muneyuki no Ason

24 The lush color
   of perennial pines
  when spring arrives
   is double-dyed again
   in deeper shades of green

Composed and presented when he was commanded[8] *to present a song*

Tsurayuki

26   The green willow,

        its threads entwined together

     until the spring,

        when the seams are unraveled

        by the blossoming flowers

Composed on the willow tree in the Great Temple of the West

Archbishop Henjō

27   Green filaments

        overhanging together

     with white droplets

        threaded like beads of dew

        on the willow in spring

[8]   By Emperor Daigo.

Composed when he heard the cry of the geese and was reminded of someone who had left for Koshi

Ōshikōchi no Mitsune

30   Spring has arrived
            and I can hear the geese
        about to leave:
            will they carry a message
            on their path of white clouds?

Composed on geese returning

Ise

31   Though the spring haze
            rises the geese are leaving
        without a glance;
            perhaps what they prefer
            are gardens without blossoms?

Topic unknown

Author unknown

32   I plucked a branch
          and now my sleeves are scented.
      Does the warbler
          think they are plum blossoms
          as it sings by my side?

33   Not the color
          but the scent—that is what
      moves me the most
          about the garden plum tree
          that someone's sleeves brushed by

34 I will not grow
    plum blossoms in my garden
  lest I be tricked
    and take them for the scent
    of the one I await

35 Since that moment
    when I briefly drew near
  the plum blossoms,
    there are those who reproach me
    for the scent on my sleeves

Composed when on a moonlit night someone said, "pick some plum blossoms," as he was about to pick them

Mitsune

40   This moonlit night
     it is hard to distinguish
    the plum blossoms:
      they can only be known
      by seeking out their scent

Composed on plum blossoms on a spring night

41   The spring night,
     its darkness is in vain:
    although it may
      hide the plum blossom's color,
      can it conceal the scent?

Song from the Empress's Song Contest in the Kanpyō Era
Dharma Master Sosei

47   It is better
        to accept that they will scatter,
    the plum blossoms;
        and yet their scent remains
        lingering on my sleeves

Topic unknown

Author unknown

48   If you scatter
        then leave me at least your scent,
    plum tree blossoms,
        to keep as a memento
        for those times I long for you

Composed when he saw that the cherry blossoms growing at a certain person's house had begun to bloom

Tsurayuki

49   Cherry blossoms
      that this year know the spring
  for the first time:
    I wish you never learned
    that blossoms always scatter

Topic unknown

Author unknown

51   I came to see
      the mountain cherry blossoms,
  but the spring haze
    at both the peak and foot
    has risen to conceal them

Composed upon seeing cherry blossoms placed in a vase before the
Somedono Empress Consort

> *The former Great Minister of the Realm*[9]

52   As the years pass,

                my age has kept increasing,

        yet even so

                when I look at the blossoms

                my sorrows disappear

Composed on seeing cherry blossoms at the Nagisa-in[10]

> *Ariwara no Narihira no Ason*

53   If in this world

                there were no such things as

        cherry blossoms,

                the sentiments of spring

                would be far more serene

---

[9]   Fujiwara no Yoshifusa. The Somedono Empress was his daughter, Fujiwara
      Akirakeiko (829–899).

[10] A residence of Prince Koretaka.

Composed upon seeing the mountain cherry blossoms

Dharma Master Sosei

55   How to describe

the beauty of the blossoms

from sight alone?

Let us each pick one out

as a gift to take home

Composed at the height of the blossoms, looking down at the capital

56   In the distance,

willows and cherry blossoms

mingle and weave

so the capital seems

covered in spring brocade

Topic unknown

Ki no Aritomo

66   I would deep-dye

my garments in the color

of the cherry,

to wear them in remembrance

when the blossoms have scattered

Composed at the Pavilion Palace Song Contest[11]

Ise

68   Cherry blossoms

in a mountain village where

no one sees you:

I wish that you would flower

after the rest have fallen

[11]   The Pavilion Palace (*Teiji no in*) was a private residence of Emperor Uda and his consort Fujiwara no Onshi after his abdication in 897. The song contest was held in 913.

VOLUME 2—SPRING SONGS 2

Topic unknown

Author unknown

69   Cherry blossoms
          in the spring haze that trails
    over the hills,
       do they reflect their passing,
       the colors that are fading?

71   Cherry blossoms—
          I love how you all scatter
    with no regrets,
       rather than living on
       until the bitter end

72 In this village
     I must lodge for the night,
   confused by the
     scattering cherry blossoms,
     having lost my way home

73 They are just like
     this evanescent world,
   the cherry blossoms;
     just as we see them flower
     already they have scattered

At the Urin-in,[12] *composed on cherry blossoms*

Dharma Master Sōku

77   Cherry blossoms,

     like you I too would scatter;

   we may flourish

     for a brief while before

     they look at us with pity

At a time when she was feeling unwell and had drawn the blinds so as not to be exposed to the wind, she saw a sprig of cherry that had lost its blossoms and composed

Fujiwara Yoruka no Ason

80   Sitting inside,

     unaware that the spring

   was passing by,

     the blossoms I awaited

     have now faded away

---

[12] Originally a residence for emperors and crown princes, it was bestowed on Archbishop Henjō in 869, and later became a temple of the Tendai sect.

At the Eastern Prince's Palace,[13] *composed upon seeing cherry blos-
soms fall and run down the stream*

Sugano no Takayo

81   From the branches,

the blossoms that had scattered

already in vain,

once fallen have become

the foam upon the water

Composed on scattering cherry blossoms

Ki no Tomonori

84   On a spring day

when the light in the sky

remains so calm,

what feelings of unease

lead the blossoms to scatter?

13   The Crown Prince's Palace.

Topic unknown

Ōtomo no Kuronushi

88   This soft rainfall
        it must be made of tears:
    for who is there
        that does not feel regret
        when cherry blossoms scatter?

Song from the Pavilion Palace Song Contest

Tsurayuki

89   In the wake
        of a wind in which blossoms
    have scattered,
        in the waterless sky
        it is waves that are rising

Composed as a spring song

Yoshimine no Munesada

91   The blossom's colors
            are hidden by the haze:
      spring mountain wind—
            if you will not reveal them,
            then steal at least their scent

Songs from the Empress's Song Contest in the Kanpyō Era

Fujiwara no Okikaze

101   Though the blossoms
            in their thousands of hues
      flower in vain,
            who could ever reproach
            the sentiments of spring?

102　　　The haze of spring
　　　　　　looks like a thousand colors
　　　　trailing over
　　　　　　the mountains as it catches
　　　　　　reflections from the blossoms

Ariwara no Motokata

103　　　Though the mountains
　　　　　　where the spring haze is rising
　　　　are far away,
　　　　　　the wind comes blowing down
　　　　　　bringing the scent of blossoms

Composed upon seeing the fading blossoms

Mitsune

104   When I look at

the blossoms, my heart too

starts to change hue;

I will not show my colors

lest they betray my thoughts

Topic unknown

Author unknown

105   To each meadow

where the bush warbler cries

I come and see

the fading of the blossoms

as they blow in the wind

Topic unknown

Ono no Komachi

113   The blossoms' color

          has now faded away,

    just as in vain

          I have aged in the world

          gazing at the long rains[14]

Composed when he visited a mountain temple

Tsurayuki

117   In my lodgings

          on the spring mountainside

    asleep at night,

          even within my dreams

          the blossoms keep on scattering

---

[14] This poem has two untranslatable puns: *nagame* (long rains, gazing) and *furu* (aging, falling).

A group of women returning from Shiga were at Hanayama[15] and were standing beneath the wisteria blossoms, and as they were about to leave he composed this and sent it to them

Archbishop Henjō

119
    A casual look

        and then they turn to leave:

    wisteria tree,

        cling to them with your blossoms

        though your branches may break

Composed when the wisteria flowers were blossoming in his garden, and he saw people stop to look at them

Mitsune

120
    In my garden

        blooming wisteria waves

    keep returning

        like those who stop to look,

        unable to pass by

---

15 Hanayama or Kazan (a different reading of the same graphs) refers to the location of Henjō's temple of Gangyōji, north of the Heian capital.

Topic unknown

Author unknown

125   On the embankment
         where the kerria has scattered
    a frog cries out,
         wishing that they had met
         when it was still in blossom

According to some people, this song is by Tachibana no Kiyotomo.

On the last day of the third month, composed upon seeing women returning from picking blossoms

Mitsune

132   Though they are not
         something that can be stopped,
    my heart is moved
         by each and every blossom
         as it scatters in vain

• 51 •

On the last day of the third month, when it was raining, he broke off
a sprig of wisteria and sent it to someone

Narihira no Ason

133   Just to pick this
              it was worth getting wet,
       knowing today
              is the last day of spring
              before the end of the year

VOLUME 3—SUMMER SONGS

Topic unknown

Author unknown

135   In my garden
           wisteria waves have blossomed
over the pond.
           When will the mountain cuckoo
           come here to cry its song?

According to some people, this song is by Kakinomoto no Hitomaro.

137   Mountain cuckoo,
           awaiting the fifth month:
let your wings spread
           and come cry to us now
           with your old voice from last year

139 Orange blossoms
   awaiting the fifth month:
 their scent recalls
   that fragrance on the sleeves
   of someone long ago

Composed upon hearing the cuckoo sing for the first time
          Sosei

143 Cuckoo bird,
   when I hear its first cries,
 for no reason
   I am filled with deep longing
   without knowing for whom

Topic unknown

Author unknown

149   Though you cry out,

        you never show your tears

     cuckoo bird:

        let me lend you my robe

        with these sleeves that are drenched

Songs from the Empress's Song Contest in the Kanpyō Era

Ki no Tomonori

153   Deep in my thoughts

        as the summer rains fall

     and the cuckoo

        cries deep into the night,

        I wonder where it goes

Tsurayuki

156
This summer night
    about to go to bed
when the cuckoo
    utters a single cry
    at the first light of day

Mibu no Tadamine

157
It seemed like dusk
    but I see dawn has come
this summer night
    on which the mountain cuckoo
    is crying without rest

On a night with a beautiful moon, composed just before daylight
Fukayabu

166 On summer nights,
   when so soon after midnight
  the dawn arrives,
   to what place in the clouds
   does the moon go to rest?

Composed on the last day of the sixth month
Mitsune

168 Down the sky road
   on which summer and autumn
  are crossing paths,
   blowing cool on one side
   the wind must be approaching

VOLUME 4—AUTUMN SONGS 1

Composed on the first day of autumn

Fujiwara no Toshiyuki no Ason

169   Though the arrival
     of autumn cannot be
   seen by the eyes,
     I was suddenly alerted
     by the sound of the wind

Topic unknown[16]

Author unknown

173   Since the first day

         the winds of autumn blew,

     by the embankment

         of the heavenly river

         every day I stand waiting

174   At the embankment,

         of the heavenly river,

     ferry master,

         if my lord were to cross

         make sure to hide the oars

[16]   This poem begins a sequence (173–182) on the topic of *Tanabata*, the festival of the Oxherd and the Weaver, lovers who were transformed into the stars Altair and Vega and condemned to meet only one night in the year, the seventh of the seventh lunar month (in autumn, by the Heian lunar calendar), when the Oxherd crosses the heavenly river (the Milky Way). This first poem is in the voice of the Weaver maid.

175 The weaver maid—
    is it so scarlet leaves
  become a bridge
    on the heavenly river
    that she waits for the autumn?

176 Longing for love
    and tonight is the night;
  let the mist rise
    on the heavenly river
    and may dawn never come

In the Kanpyō era, on the seventh night, when the emperor com-
manded the men in the palace to compose songs, there was one who
could not, so he composed in his place

Tomonori

177   Seeking the ford
        of the heavenly river
    amid white waves
        when before I could cross
        it was suddenly dawn

Composed at dawn on the seventh night

Minamoto no Muneyuki no Ason

182   "It is time now"
        and as we say goodbye,
    before I have
        crossed the heavenly river,
        my sleeves are already drenched

Topic unknown

Author unknown

184   Seeing the light
        of the moon as it seeps
    through the branches,
        the melancholy season
        of autumn has arrived

186   I know autumn
        does not come just for me,
    yet when I hear
        the voices of the crickets
        I feel nothing but sadness

192   It seems the night

        is moving toward midnight,

  as cries of geese

      can be heard in the sky

      where the moon has appeared[17]

Composed at the Prince Koresada[18] Mansion Song Contest

                          Ōe no Chisato

193   Watching the moon,

      the thousand things I feel

  turn to sadness,

      though I know that the autumn

      is not only for me

[17] This poem also appears in *Man'yōshū*, vol. 9 (#1701), where it is attributed to Prince Yuge (d. 699).

[18] A son of Emperor Kōkō and brother of Emperor Uda, he died in 903.

On a night after parting from someone, composed upon hearing a grasshopper cry

Fujiwara no Tadafusa

196   Grasshopper,

         do not cry with such sorrow;

     like the autumn nights[19]

         your complaints may be long

         but mine are all the more

Topic unknown

Author unknown

201   In the autumn

         fields I became confused

     and lost my way:

         I will go to seek lodging

         where the pine crickets cry

[19]   Autumn nights are the longest, by convention.

205

In the evenings
    when the cicadas cry,
no one visits
    this hut up on the mountain
    except for the autumn wind

210

Through the spring haze
    in the distance the geese
that flew away
    have now returned to cry
    above the autumn mists

211 The night is cold
    without a robe to share,
  as wild geese cry
    and the bush clover's leaves
    have begun to change color

According to some people, this song is by Kakinomoto no Hitomaro.

A song from the Empress's Song Contest in the Kanpyō Era
         Fujiwara no Sugane no Ason

212 The approaching ship,
    its sails rising like voices
  on the autumn wind,
    is a flock of geese crossing
    the harbor of the heavens

Songs from the Prince Koresada Mansion Song Contest

Tadamine

214   The mountain hut
    is especially lonely
in the autumn,
    awaking to the sound
    of the cry of the deer

Author unknown

215   Deep in the hills
    treading through scarlet leaves,
a deer cries out,
    and in its voice I hear
    all the sadness of autumn

Topic unknown

216   Perhaps it is

     in despair at the autumn

   clover's passing,

     that the deer's cry resounds

     at the base of the mountain?

217   Although our eyes

     cannot see the deer

   as it cavorts

     and prances in the clover,

     we can still hear its cry

Topic unknown

Author unknown

221   Are those the tears

        shed by the crying geese

    crossing the sky,

        the dewdrops on the clover

        by this house where I languish?

224   I want to walk

        across the fields of scattering

    clover blossoms

        soaked by the dew and frost

        though the night may be late[20]

[20] A similar poem appears in *Man'yōshū*, vol. 10 (#2252), in the section "Autumn Exchanges" as one of a sequence of eight poems under the heading "Comparing to Dew."

Composed at the Prince Koresada Mansion Song Contest

Funya no Asayasu

225 On the autumn fields

   the fallen white dewdrops

look just like pearls

   as they hang threaded through

   the cobweb of a spider

Topic unknown

Archbishop Henjō

226 It was your name

   that led me to pick you

maiden flower:

   do not let it be known

   I have strayed from the path

When traveling to Nara to Archbishop Henjō's house,[21] composed when he saw a maiden flower on Otokoyama (Male Mountain)

Furu no Imamichi

227   Maiden flowers,
        I have always walked by them
    with indifference,
        given that where they grow
        has the name of Male Mountain

Topic unknown

Ono no Yoshiki

229   Spending the night
        on a field with so many
    maiden flowers,
        people will call me fickle
        through no fault of my own

[21] At the time, Henjō lived at Isonokami Temple in Nara.

Composed and presented at the Suzaku Palace Maiden Flower Contest

Minister of the Left[22]

230   Maiden flower,

      blown about in the wind

   on the autumn fields,

      to whom will she entrust

      her single steadfast heart?

Topic unknown

Author unknown

245   The wild grasses

      that in the spring I saw

   as only green

      in the autumn have turned

      to multicolored blossoms

---

[22] Fujiwara no Tokihira (871–909).

247   With moon flowers

       I want to dye my garments,

  and I care not

       that their colors will fade

       when soaked in morning dew [23]

When the Ninna Emperor was still a prince, he came to see the Furu waterfalls, and on the way he stayed at the house of Henjō's mother, where the garden was designed as a wild autumn field, and as they were conversing he composed and presented

Henjō

248   Has the owner

       grown old and the estate

  been neglected,

       that both garden and hedge

       are now just autumn fields?

---

[23] This poem also appears in *Man'yōshū*, vol. 7 (#1351), in the section "Metaphorical Poems" as one of seventeen poems under the heading "Comparing to Grass."

VOLUME 5—AUTUMN SONGS 2

A song from the Prince Koresada Mansion Song Contest

Funya no Yasuhide

250   Both grass and trees

have their changes of color,

but on the sea

the blossoms of the waves

will never know the autumn

Composed at an autumn song contest

Ki no Yoshimochi

251   Since evergreen

hills see no change in color,

perhaps it is

through the sound of the wind

that they hear of the autumn?

Composed at the Prince Koresada Mansion Song Contest

Toshiyuki no Ason

257   How can it be

                that from the single color

        of the white dew

                the autumn leaves are dyed

                into thousands of hues?[24]

Topic unknown

Author unknown

259   Perhaps it is

                because the dew in autumn

        falls in colors,

                that tree leaves on the mountain

                turn to thousands of hues?

---

[24]   The theory underlying this and the following poems is that dew causes the autumn leaves to color. The emphasis on "white" dew is based on the association of the color white with autumn according to the classical Chinese theory of the five elements.

When he went to the land of Yamato, composed upon seeing the mist rising over Mount Saho

Ki no Tomonori

265 I wonder for

    whose eyes is this brocade

  that the autumn mist

    has risen to conceal

    on the side of Mount Saho?

A song from the Prince Koresada Mansion Song Contest

Author unknown

266 The autumn mists

    should not rise up this morning,

  so I may see

    Mount Saho's scarlet leaves

    if only from a distance

In the Kanpyō era, when requested to compose on chrysanthemum
blossoms

Toshiyuki no Ason

269   In the distance

above the clouds I see

chrysanthemums

appearing to my eyes

just like stars in the heavens

This song was from a time when he was still not allowed in the inner
court and was summoned to present

In the same era, at the chrysanthemum contest where a model of a
sand beach was built and songs were offered together with chrysan-
themums.[25] *Composed on chrysanthemums on Fukiage Beach*

Sugawara no Ason

272   In the autumn wind

at Fukiage beach,

white chrysanthemums:

Are they blossoms or not?

Or are they waves of foam?

[25]   The first sentence in the headnote applies to the following four poems (272–275),
and the second just to *Kokinshū* 272 (hereafter cited as *KKS*).

*Composed on a model of a person walking through chrysanthemums
to the dwelling of an immortal*

Sosei

273 In the brief while

     the dew from the chrysanthemums

   along the path

     took to dry on my robes

     I spent one thousand years

*Composed on a model of a person beside chrysanthemum blossoms
waiting for another person*

Tomonori

274 Watching blossoms

     as I waited for someone,

   for a moment

     I was sure I had seen

     the sleeves of their white robe

Composed on chrysanthemums growing on a model of Ōsawa Pond

275   I had thought there
      was just a single blossom;
    so who planted
      another in the depths
      of the Ōsawa Pond?

Topic unknown

           Author unknown

284   The scarlet leaves
      flow on Tatsuta River;
    on the divine
      and sacred Mount Mimuro
      autumn rain must be falling

A variant has "The scarlet leaves flow on Asuka River . . ."

286 The scarlet leaves
   that scatter at the mercy
 of the autumn wind,
   wandering without aim
   in the midst of my sadness

287 Autumn has come
   and my garden is covered
 in scarlet leaves,
   with no path leading through
   since no one comes to visit

289 The autumn moon
     illuminates the hillside
  so clearly,
     perhaps so we can count
     the falling scarlet leaves?

290 The blowing wind
     takes the form of a robe
  of many hues
     that are the leaves of autumn
     scattering from the trees

Fujiwara no Sekio

291   The warp of frost
       and the weft of the dew
  are weak indeed:
      the mountain brocades scatter
      as soon as they are woven

In Kitayama, composed when he was about to pick some autumn leaves before leaving

Tsurayuki

297   Seen by no one
      as they scatter away,
  the scarlet leaves
      that lie deep in the hills
      are like brocade at night

Presented when asked to compose on the topic of a picture on a screen in the Pavilion Palace in which a man who is about to cross a river has stopped his horse beneath a tree from which scarlet leaves are falling

Mitsune

305   I will stop here
      and cross after I watch
    the scarlet leaves:
      though they fall like the rain
      the waters will not rise

Composed on an excursion to pick mushrooms with Archbishop Henjō

Dharma Master Sosei

309   I will return
      with my sleeves full of fallen
    scarlet leaves
      to show to those who say
      that autumn is now gone

*In the Kanpyō era, when commanded to present an old song, he
wrote down a song about scarlet leaves flowing in the Tatsuta River,
and composed another in the same spirit*

Okikaze

310   It was the sight

     of colors in the water

    flowing down from

      the hills which made me think

      that autumn is now gone

Composed on the end of autumn thinking of the Tatsuta River

Tsurayuki

311   Year after year

     as the scarlet leaves flow

    down to the mouth

      of the Tatsuta River

      the autumn comes to harbor

Composed on the last day of the Long Month, by the great well

312   Is it the voice
                of the deer crying out
          in the evening
                darkness of Mount Ogura
                that marks the end of autumn?

Composed on the last day of the Long Month.
                                    Mitsune

313   If I knew the
                path I would go in search
          of scarlet leaves
                and tie them as an offering
                to the departed autumn

VOLUME 6—WINTER SONGS

Topic unknown

Author unknown

314 Tatsuta River

   seems woven from brocade

  in the tenth month,

    with the rains of winter

    as the warp and the weft

Composed as a winter song

Minamoto no Muneyuki no Ason

315 The mountain hut

   is all the more lonely

  in the winter,

    when people stay away

    and the grass is all withered

Topic unknown

Author unknown

316
So cold the light
of the moon in the sky
that the water
in which it was reflected
was the first to freeze over

317
As evening comes
I feel cold in my sleeves:
In Yoshino,
the fair hills of Yoshino,
it seems that snow is falling[26]

---

[26] A similar poem appears in *Man'yōshū*, vol. 10 (#2319), in the section "Winter Miscellaneous Songs" as one of nine poems under the heading "Composing on Snow."

322   My garden is
            covered in fallen snow,
      without a path
            on which to wander through,
            since no one ever visits

Composed on falling snow

Kiyohara no Fukayabu

330   Still in winter,
            and yet from the sky blossoms
      come scattering.
            Perhaps beyond the clouds
            the spring has now arrived?

Composed on snow that had fallen and covered the trees

Tsurayuki

331   Winter-hidden,
            I could not picture them,
        yet through the trees
            I now see them as blossoms,
            the snowflakes that are falling

When he went to the land of Yamato, composed upon seeing the snow falling

Sakanoue no Korenori

332   In the early morning
            they look like rays of moonlight
        shining at dawn,
            white snowflakes as they fall
            in the village of Yoshino

Topic unknown

Author unknown

333   Still not melted
            yet I wish it fell again;
    the sight of snow
            will be a rare thing indeed
            once the spring haze arrives

334   The plum blossoms
            do not seem like themselves,
    as distant skies
            are clouded by the snow
            that is falling all around

According to some people, this song is by Kakinomoto Hitomaro.

Composed on snow falling upon plum blossoms

Ono Takamura no Ason

335 Though the color
  of the blossoms is hidden
amid the snow,
  may they at least be fragrant
  so people can distinguish

Composed at the end of the year

Ariwara no Motokata

339 As always,
  once again as the year
comes to an end,
  my age keeps on increasing
  just like the falling snow

A song from the Empress's Song Contest in the Kanpyō Era

Author unknown

340   As the snow falls

         and the year draws to a close,

     this is the time

         to look at the pine tree

         that does not lose its leaves

Composed at the end of the year.

Harumichi no Tsuraki

341   Say "yesterday,"

         and we live through today

     as the Asuka[27]

         river flows swiftly by

         with the months and the days

[27] This poem includes a conventional pun on the name of the river *Asuka* and *asu,* which means "tomorrow."

VOLUME 7—FELICITOUS SONGS

Topic unknown

Author unknown

343 May our lord live

    a thousand, eight thousand ages

  until pebbles

    are transformed into rocks

    and are covered in moss[28]

344 Counting the grains

    of sand upon the shore

  of the great sea

    may they truly become

    our lord's one thousand years

[28] This poem, with a slight variation in the first line, is the lyrics of the modern
Japanese national anthem.

*Composed for the celebration of the Horikawa Minister's[29] fortieth
birthday, at his home on the ninth avenue*

Ariwara no Narihira no Ason

349   Cherry blossoms,

      scatter up into clouds

    and thus obscure

      the path on which they say

      is the approach of old age

*Composed and written upon a screen for the celebration of Prince
Motoyasu's[30] seventieth birthday*

Ki no Tsurayuki

352   When spring arrives,

      the first flowers to bloom

    are plum blossoms:

      may they serve to adorn

      my lord's one thousand years

---

[29] Fujiwara no Mototsune (836–891).

[30] A son of Emperor Ninmyō, Prince Motoyasu died in 902.

Composed during a visit to the newborn Eastern Prince

Fujiwara no Yoruka no Ason

364   The sun rising

     over the lofty peaks

   of Mount Kasuga

    will illuminate all

    and will never be clouded[31]

---

[31] The "Eastern Prince" of the headnote refers to the crown prince, as does the "sun" in the poem. "Mount Kasuga" is the ancestral shrine of the Fujiwara lineage, the crown prince's maternal relatives.

VOLUME 8—FAREWELL SONGS

At Prince Sadatoki's[32] *house, when Fujiwara no Kiyō*[33] *was leaving
for Ōmi, composed on the night of his farewell banquet*

Ki no Toshisada

369   Today we part

         and though I know tomorrow

    we meet in Ōmi,

        is the late night the reason

        for this dew on my sleeves?[34]

Composed and sent to someone who was going to Koshi

370   I know its name

        is the "Hill of Return"

    but if I see

        you leave through the spring haze

        I will still feel abandoned[35]

---

[32] A son of Emperor Seiwa.

[33] A midranking court official who served as governor of Yamato.

[34] This poem features a pun on the name Ōmi (*Afumi*) and the verb "to meet"
(*afu*).

[35] This poem includes a pun on the name of a mountain in Koshi called
"Kaeruyama," which can be interpreted as "Hill of Return."

Composed when someone close to him who had been away in Koshi
returned to the capital after many years and left again soon after

Ōshikōchi no Mitsune

382   "Hill of Return"—

        why do they call it that?

     Perhaps it means

        when at last he comes back

        he hardly stays at all?

When Fujiwara no Koreoka went to Musashi no Suke, composed
while bidding farewell, on the topic of crossing Meeting Hill

Tsurayuki

390   People cross it

        also when they depart:

     this "Meeting Hill"

        has a name that is full

        of nothing but false hope

When someone came to visit him in Hanayama, in the evening, composed when they were about to leave

Henjō

392   In the evening light,

      I wish my hedge appeared

   to be a mountain

      you would not dare to cross

      and so were forced to stay

After climbing the hill, on the way down, composed when his companions were saying farewell to him

Dharma Master Yūsen

393   I will entrust

      my farewells to the cherries

   of the mountain:

      let the blossoms decide

      to detain you or not

VOLUME 9—TRAVEL SONGS

Composed in the realm of the Tang while gazing at the moon
Abe no Nakamaro

406 When I look up
    at the heavenly plain
I see the moon
    that rose back in Kasuga
    over Mikasa Hill

Regarding this song, long ago when Nakamaro was sent to the Tang to study, he was unable to return for many years, but when he was at last commanded to accompany back an envoy from this land, the people of that land held a farewell banquet for him at a place called Mingzhou by the sea. As night fell, and they watched a beautiful moon rise, he is said to have composed this.

When he was exiled to the land of Oki, he boarded the ship and when it was about to depart, he sent this to someone at court

Ono Takamura no Ason

407   Fisherman's boat—
                go and tell them back home
          I have sailed forth
                on the plain of the ocean
                bound for the eighty islands

Topic unknown

Author unknown

409   Faintly at dawn
                through the bay of Akashi's
          morning mists
                the ship for which I yearn
                rows out beyond the islands

According to some people this song is by Kakinomoto no Hitomaro.

He went to the East, taking one or two friends with him. In the land of Mikawa they reached a place called Yatsuhashi, and in the vicinity of the river, seeing some irises blossoming beautifully, he sat down beneath the shade of a tree and using the five letters of "iris" (ka–ki–tu–ha–ta)[36] to begin each measure, he composed on feelings of love

Ariwara no Narihira no Ason

410   This Chinese robe

   that I have worn since leaving

 my wife behind,

   like my thoughts has become

   unraveled on my journey

---

[36] The poem is too famous not to translate, but the acrostic cannot be reproduced in English: *karakoromo / kitutu narenisi / tuma si areba / harubaru kinuru / tabi wo si zo omofu.* The poem also contains several puns: *kitutu* and *kinuru* (have come, have been wearing), *tuma* (wife, hem), *harubaru* (a long way, stretched out).

Upon reaching the Sumida River, which divides the lands of Musashi and Shimotsufusa, he felt a strong longing for the capital, got down to sit by the river for a while, and as he was gazing around pensively and lamenting the immense distance he had come, the ferryman said, "we need to board quickly—the sun is about to go down," and as they got on the boat to cross the river everyone was depressed and in that moment when everyone was thinking of someone from the capital, suddenly he saw a white bird with a red beak and red legs wandering at the edge of the river. Since it was a bird unlike those seen in the capital, no one knew what it was, so he inquired of the ferryman what kind of bird it was, and when he heard that he had answered, "that is a capital bird," he composed

411   If to your name
                   you are true then I ask you,
           capital bird:
                   Is the one whom I love
                   alive or is she gone?

VOLUME 11—LOVE SONGS 1

Topic unknown

Author unknown

469   In the fifth month
     the irises can sense
    the cuckoo's cry;
     but I can find no sense
     in this love that I feel[37]

Dharma Master Sosei

470   Hearing rumors
     of white dew on chrysanthemums
    falling awake
     all night and all day hoping
     to perish in the sunlight

[37] This poem includes a pun on *ayame* (pattern, logic, sense) and *ayamegusa* (iris—a different variety from the *kakitsubata* iris in Narihira's poem KKS 410).

Ki no Tsurayuki

471   Over the rocks
        of the Yoshino River
    the water flows
        as rapidly as I
        began to fall in love

Fujiwara no Kachion

472   So too the boat
        on a course where white waves
    leave no traces,
        has nothing to rely on
        but the signs in the wind

Ariwara no Motokata

474   Time and again
     it constantly returns
this love I feel
     for one who is far away
     like white waves in the offing

Tsurayuki

475   Such is the way
     of affairs in this world:
the one I love,
     like whispers in the wind,
     my eyes will never see

On the day of an archery contest at the riding grounds of the Impe-
rial Guards of the Right, through the lower blinds of the carriage
that was standing across from him, for just a moment he glimpsed
the face of a woman, composed this and sent it to her

Ariwara no Narihira no Ason

476   In love with one

                  I neither did not see

            nor truly saw,

                  confused I spent the day

                  gazing at the long rains

Response

Author unknown

477   Why be confused

                  by whether you knew me

            or knew me not?

                  Surely what you should know

                  is if your love is true

When he went to the Kasuga Festival, he saw a woman who had come to enjoy the sights, and after inquiring where she lived, had this sent to her

Mibu no Tadamine

478   At Kasuga,

          walking through fields of snow,

      like the young grass

          that was growing beneath,

          I caught a glimpse of you

When he went to a place where people were picking flowers, composed later and sent to someone he saw there

Tsurayuki

479   Mountain cherries

          through the gaps in the haze

      faintly I saw

          only the briefest glimpse

          of the one whom I love

Topic unknown

Ōshikōchi no Mitsune

481   Since the moment

     when I heard the faint cries

   of the first geese,

    all I can do is yearn

    as I gaze at the sky

Tsurayuki

482   I can no more

     meet her than reach the clouds

   in the distance

    where the thunder resounds

    as my longing continues

Topic unknown

Author unknown

498 From the branches
    at the top of the plum tree
  in my garden
    just like the warbler sings
    so should I cry with longing

499 O cuckoo bird
    of the reed-pulling mountain,
  are you like me
    longing for him so much
    you cannot fall asleep?

501   It seems the gods
              did not listen to me
        when I asked them
              by Mitarashi River
              to wash away my longing

502   If there were no
              such things as words to move us,
        what would we do
              in order to restrain
              the confusion of love?

516   Night after night,
        I cannot find a place
for my pillow,
        how did I sleep that night
        I saw you in my dreams?

521   Longing for one
        who loves not in return,
the only response
        to my lamenting cries
        was the echo from the hills

522   More pointless than
                doing sums on the surface
        of a river
                is to keep loving someone
                who loves not in return

527   My pillow flows
                on a river of tears
        as I float on
                restlessly in my sleep
                and unable to dream

542   When spring arrives
           and the ice melts away
       leaving nothing,
           so I wish that your heart
           would open up to mine

543   When dawn arrives,
           like the crickets I cry
       all the day long
           and at night like the fireflies
           I continue to burn

545   When evening comes,
      my sleeves that were already
   hard to keep dry
      become all the more drenched
      with falling autumn dew

551   Just like the snow
      that covers the sedge roots
   deep in the hills
      will eventually melt,
      I too from love will perish[38]

---

[38] A similar poem appears in *Man'yōshū*, vol. 8 (#1655), in the section "Winter Exchange Songs," attributed to Mikuni no Mahito Hitotari (fl. early eighth century).

VOLUME 12—LOVE SONGS 2

Topic unknown

Ono no Komachi

552   Did I see him
          because I fell asleep
      thinking of him?
          Had I known I was dreaming
          I would not have awoken

553   In a slumber
            I saw the one I love,
        and ever since
            I have begun to trust
            in these things they call dreams

554   When my longing
            is at its most intense,
        in the pitch dark
            night I reverse my robes
            and wear them inside out

*At a memorial service in the Lower Izumo Temple, he composed a
song based on the sermon of the Dharma Master Shinsei and had it
sent to Ono no Komachi*

Abe no Kiyoyuki no Ason

556   These white pearldrops
       that cannot be contained
     within my sleeves,
       are the tears from my eyes
       that cannot see my love

Response

Komachi

557   Those are fickle
       tears if they turn to pearls
     upon your sleeves:
       mine are like rushing rapids
       that no dam can restrain

Songs from the Empress's Song Contest in the Kanpyō Era

Fujiwara no Toshiyuki Ason

558   Lying asleep

    tormented by this longing,

I wish the path

    of dreams on which we meet

    were that of the real world

559   In Sumi Bay

    waves come to shore as night

is approaching,

    but still you keep avoiding

    the paths within my dreams

Ki no Tomonori

562   When evening comes,

though I burn like the fireflies,

is it perhaps

because she sees no light

that she remains so distant?

563   Even colder

than the frost that has covered

the bamboo grass

is the touch of my sleeves

as I sleep all alone

564
Frost settles on
the chrysanthemum hedge
in my garden,
then melts away yet always
returns, just like my longing

565
Like the swaying
gemweed that hides beneath
the river shoals
my love is of a kind
I can reveal to no one

Fujiwara no Okikaze

567   Longing for you,
        I have completely filled
      my bed with tears,
          and my body exhausted
        is floating like a buoy

568   This dying life
          could perhaps be revived,
        if you just tried
            for the briefest of instants
          to say that you will meet me

Author unknown

570   Without respite,
           whether I sleep or wake
       I feel longing;
           where should I send my heart
           so that it may forget you?

571   If love's despair
           caused my spirit to wander,
       would I be known
           as the hollow remains
           of one who lived for nothing?

Topic unknown

Tsurayuki

574   Does dew also
     fall on the path of dreams?
   All the night long
     I wander back and forth
     my drenched sleeves never drying

Dharma Master Sosei

575   During the night,
     in vain I saw in dreams
   the one I love,
     then from my morning bed
     was too depressed to rise

Tadamine

601 Like the white clouds
    that part over the peaks
  when the wind blows,
    just as indifferent are
    your feelings toward me

602 If my body
    were such it could transform
  into moonlight,
    would she who is indifferent
    look upon me with longing?

Mitsune

608   It was surely
     because I fell asleep
   thinking of you
     that I saw in my dream
     what my heart so desired

Tadamine

609   That which I find
     even more disappointing
   than life itself,
     is waking from a dream
     before it has concluded

Mitsune

612
Who else but me
> has to bear with such sadness?
Even the Oxherd
> does not see out the year
> without meeting his love[39]

Tomonori

615
Who needs this life?
> Like the dew it means nothing.
With no regrets
> I would gladly exchange it
> if only I could meet her

[39] See the Tanabata sequence (poems 173–182).

VOLUME 13—LOVE SONGS 3

On the first day of the third month, after conversing with someone in secret, as it was raining softly, he composed this and had it sent

Ariwara no Narihira no Ason

616   Neither awake

          nor capable of sleep

I spent the night

          and then all day long gazing

          at the falling spring rain

Composed and sent to a woman who served at Narihira no Ason's house

Toshiyuki no Ason

617   I watch the rain

          as it falls in this swelling

river of tears

          and my sleeves become drenched

          with no way to meet you

Composed as a response in place of the woman

Narihira no Ason

618   To drench your sleeves

     all you need are the shallows;

   I might trust you

     were you to float downstream

     on your river of tears

Topic unknown

Author unknown

621   As lonely nights

     accumulate just like

   falling white snow

     I wish that I myself

     could also melt away

According to some people, this song is by Kakinomoto no Hitomaro.

Motokata

626   Just like the waves
          are drawn to the shore where
we never meet,
      I gaze upon the beach
      in reproach as I return

Author unknown

627   Are they perhaps
          like the waves that rise up
before the wind,
      the rumors that arise
      without us having met?

Miharu no Arisuke

629   Tatsuta River,
       where rumors have arisen
  without reason
     yet will not end until
     we meet on the other shore

Tsurayuki

633   Though I hide it,
      when my longing becomes
  too much to bear,
     like the moon from the hills
    I come out to see her

Author unknown

634   All this longing,
        and tonight at long last
at Meeting Pass
        may the cockerel at dawn
        make sure to never cry

Ono no Komachi

635   The autumn nights
        are long in name alone:
we scarcely met,
        and barely said a word
        before night turned to dawn

Ōshikōchi no Mitsune

636

> I never thought
>> that they were always long:
> Since ages past
>> the length of autumn nights
>> depends on whom one meets

Author unknown

637

> As the first light
>> becomes gradually brighter,
> it feels so sad
>> to untangle our robes
>> and part from one another

Fujiwara Kunitsune no Ason

638 As dawn arrives
    I know it is that time,
  but why is it
    I cannot find the words
    to say the things I feel?

Songs from the Empress's Song Contest in the Kanpyō Era
Toshiyuki no Ason

639 As dawn arrives
    I make my way back home
  beneath the rain,
    as it drenches my sleeves
    together with my tears

Utsuku

640

Full of regret

    when we part at first light,

and it is I

    who long before the cockerel

    have now begun to cry

Author unknown

641

Was it real

    or a dream, cuckoo bird,

when the morning

    dew awoke us at dawn

    and you cried as we parted?

When Narihira no Ason went to the land of Ise he met with the shrine priestess in secret, and the next morning, while he thought about what to do without a messenger, this arrived from the woman

Author unknown

645
Did you come here?
    Or did I go to you?
I do not know.
    Was it real or a dream?
    Was I asleep or awake?

Response

Narihira no Ason

646
In the gloom
    of darkness in my heart
I was confused.
    Whether real or a dream
    let the world now decide

Topic unknown

Komachi

656 In reality

   I know it must be so,

  but it is hard

   when even in my dreams

   you continue to avoid me

657 If your love has

   no end you will come

  to me at night

   on the path of my dreams

   where no one can reproach you

VOLUME 14—LOVE SONGS 4

Topic unknown

Fujiwara no Tadayuki

680   I do not care

if you meet other people

or you do not,

like the peak of Mount Fuji

my love just keeps on burning

Ise

681   Even in dreams

not wanting to seem too

eager to meet,

and morning after morning

wincing at my reflection

Author unknown

682   Like the white waves
             flowing between the rocks
        always return,
             so too I never tire
             of hoping I will see you

Tomonori

684   Cherry blossoms
             in the spring haze that trails
        over the hills,
             just like I look at them
             I never tire of you

Topic unknown

Author unknown

689   With a single
         robe on a narrow mat,
    are you perhaps
         yearning for me tonight,
         maiden of Uji bridge?

690   Will you come here
         or should I go to you?
    As we waver
         and the moon starts to wane,
         I sleep with open doors

Dharma Master Sosei

691 Since you told me

   you were coming to see me,

  through this long month

   at night I have been waiting

   to see the moon at dawn

Fukayabu

698 I wonder who

   had the brilliant idea

  to call this "loving"?

   A more appropriate word

   would surely have been "dying"

When Fujiwara no Toshiyuki no Ason was seeing a woman who lived in Narihira no Ason's household, he sent a letter with the words, "I promise to come soon, but I am worried it will rain," and upon hearing he had said this, [Narihira] composed in place of the woman

Ariwara no Narihira no Ason

705   Since I cannot

      ask whether you love me

    or love me not,

      the rain which knows my thoughts

      continues to increase

Topic unknown

Author unknown

708   It is just like

      the fishfolk roasting salt

    in Suma bay

      when the wind blows the smoke

      in another direction

Dharma Master Sosei

714

Like the tree leaves
    in the hills change their colors
in the autumn wind
    I wonder if his heart
    is also going to change?

Author unknown

723

Could I ever
    forget the way my heart
did love you so,
    its first blossoms so deeply
    dyed in colors of scarlet?

*When he was seeing someone in secret, it was difficult to meet them,
so while walking in the vicinity of their house he composed and sent
this on hearing the cries of the geese*

Ōtomo no Kuronushi

735   At a time when

     I think of you with longing,

   I wonder if

     you knew that the first geese

     were crying as they passed?

*When the Minister of the Right was no longer living there, she col-
lected all the letters that she had received from him long ago, and
composed and sent this when she returned them*

Imperial Handmaid Fujiwara Yoruka no Ason

736   These leaves of words

     that you entrusted me

   I now return;

     Since time has passed I find

     no place for them or me

Response

The Imperial Kinsman Minister of the Right[40]

737   If this is it,

     I will gather the leaves

   of words returned,

     and although they were mine

     will treat them as your keepsake

Topic unknown

Author unknown

739   "Please wait," I say

     "and stay to sleep a while"

   yet still he leaves . . .

     May the legs of his horse

     trip on my garden's bridge!

[40] Minamoto no Yoshiari.

Topic unknown

Sakai no Hitozane

743 How could the sky
    serve as a keepsake for
  the one I love?
    And yet still I continue
    to gaze into the distance

Author unknown

744 What can I do
    with a keepsake until
  we meet again,
    when even if we meet
    I will receive no comfort?

When he met most secretly with someone who was closely guarded by her parents, while they were conversing, she was advised her parents were calling her, and just as he was hurrying to leave she took off her outer robe and gave it to him. Later, when he returned the robe, he composed:

Okikaze

745 What you gave me

    as a keepsake until

  we meet again,

    now by my tears is made

    a sunken robe of seaweed

Topic unknown

Author unknown

746 The keepsake too

    has now become my torment;

  without it here

    perhaps there would be moments

    in which I could forget

VOLUME 15—LOVE SONGS 5

*After he had started meeting someone who lived in the west wing of
the Gojō Empress's palace, in the tenth month she moved to a differ-
ent location. Although he was able to find out her new whereabouts
it was not possible to visit her, so in spring of the following year
when the plums were in blossom, on a night with a beautiful moon,
he felt nostalgia for the previous year and returned to the west wing
of the palace, and after spending the night lying on the floor until the
moon had set, he composed*

Ariwara no Narihira no Ason

747   Is this not that
      moon? Is this spring not that
    spring of last year?
     It seems that only I
     am the one that I was

Topic unknown

Ise

756   It is fitting
      that when I think of him,
    the moon's face
     reflected on my sleeve
     becomes covered in tears

Author unknown

757   Not in autumn
              and still these white dewdrops
       keep on falling,
              the tears upon my pillow
              on which I cannot sleep

761   At dawn the snipe
              beats its wings, beating them
       one hundred times,
              and so it is I count
              the nights you do not come

Archbishop Henjō

770   Around my house
    all paths have disappeared
beneath the growth,
    while I waited for someone
    who long ago lost interest

771   "I will come soon"
    he said before he left
on that morning,
    and now from dawn to dusk
    I cry with the cicadas

Author unknown

772   "Perhaps he'll come?"
       but I know he will not,
   as the cicadas
       are crying in the evening,
       and I still stand here waiting

774   He will not come,
       now I know that, and yet
   still I forget
       and wonder when this waiting
       will ever come to an end

Topic unknown

Ono no Komachi

782   This is the time,
                   when I grow old beneath
            the falling rain
                       and the leaves of your words
                   begin to change their colors

Response

Ono no Sadaki

783   If my feelings
                   for you were truly like
            leaves on the trees,
                       they would scatter away
                   at the whim of the wind

*When Narihira no Ason was living with Ki no Aritsune's daughter,
something happened for him to resent her, and for a while he would
visit in the morning and leave in the evening, so she composed and
sent this*

784   It seems you are,
                  like the heavenly clouds,
              drifting away
                  and yet you linger still
                  clearly within my sight

Response

                                    Narihira no Ason

785   If I'm drifting
                  back and forth through the sky
              it is because
                  on this hill where I live
                  the wind is so severe

Topic unknown

Author unknown

795   Within the hearts
        of people in this world
there grow blossoms
        that are of such a color
        as is easily dyed

796   There is nothing
        as hateful as one's heart;
were it not moved
        by colors there would be
        no regret when love fades

Komachi

797

Fading unseen
    yet still showing their colors,
are the blossoms
    that grow within the hearts
    of people in this world

Dharma Master Sosei

799

What can I do
    when someone I love starts
to fade away,
    but see them as I view
    the blossoms when they scatter?

Author unknown

820   Worse than the rain
        that falls on autumn leaves,
is the sadness
        when listening to the words
        of feelings that have changed

821   The autumn wind
        continues to blow over
Musashi fields,
        and in the end the color
        of all the leaves has changed

Komachi

822　Just like the crops
　　　　in the fields meet their end
　　in the autumn wind,
　　　　so I think of myself
　　　　about to waste away

Taira no Sadafumi

823　And in the end
　　　　when the autumn wind turns over
　　the kudzu leaves,
　　　　I see their hidden side
　　　　and am filled with reproach

Author unknown

825   The Uji Bridge
                is broken and abandoned
          and I forlorn
                ever since you last crossed
                so many years ago

Sakanoue no Korenori

826   Waiting for you
                is taking as long as
          Nagara Bridge,
                and all this time I yearn
                the years are passing by

Tomonori

827 Floating along,
    if only I were foam
  that melts away,
    since I have no hope left
    in this current of tears

Author unknown

828 Flowing between
    the Imose Lovers Hills
  as the tears fall
    in the Yoshino River
    love goes on in this world

VOLUME 16—LAMENT SONGS

When the Horikawa Great Minister passed away, composed after his cremation on Mount Fukakusa

Priest Shōen

831
I sought comfort
by looking upon his
fleeting body;
If only now the smoke
would rise on Mount Fukakusa!

Kamutsuke no Mineo

832
O cherry trees
of Fukakusa Fields,
if you truly
have feelings, this is the year
to dye your blossoms black

■ 181 ■

Composed when Ki no Tomonori died

Ki no Tsurayuki

838   I do not know
                what I will do tomorrow,
        but for today
                until the sun goes down
                I think of him in sadness

Mibu no Tadamine

839   With four seasons
                why did he have to die
        in the autumn,
                when we are filled with longing
                even seeing the living?

In the autumn when the Kawara Minister passed away, when he visited the house and saw that the autumn leaves were still not colored, he composed and sent in to the house

>   *The Imperial Kinsman Minister of the Right*[41]

848   Is it because

                   they were bereaved so suddenly,

           the autumn leaves,

                   that in their master's absence

                   the garden has no colors?

In the summer, one year after Fujiwara Takatsune no Ason had passed away, composed upon hearing the cry of the cuckoo

>   *Tsurayuki*

849   As I'm startled

                   this morning by the cry

           of the cuckoo,

                   it was this time last year

                   our lord bid us farewell

---

[41]   Minamoto no Yoshiari.

Composed when he was about to die

Fujiwara no Koremoto

860   Why did I think

        that the morning dew was

impermanent?

        Just because I myself

        did not lie on the grass

Composed when he was ill and becoming weaker

Narihira no Ason

861   I always knew

        that in the end I would

travel this path

        and yet I never thought

        that time would be today

VOLUME 17—MISCELLANEOUS SONGS 1

Topic unknown

Author unknown

863   It seems the dew
              is falling down upon me—
          is it the drops
              from the oars of the boat
              on the river of heaven?

864   As we enjoy
              this gathering tonight,
          to end it now
              would feel like we were rending
              robes of Chinese brocade

Composed when he saw the Gosechi Dancers

Yoshimine no Munesada

872   Heavenly winds—

blow forth and close the path

across the clouds,

so these beautiful maidens

may stay with us a while

*On the morning of the Gosechi Festival, he saw a fallen hairbead,
asked whose it was, and composed*

The Kawara Minister of the Left

873   I asked the bead

to whom it did belong,

yet no answer:

and so my only choice

is be moved by them all

*Composed when Ōshikōchi no Mitsune was visiting and commented
that the moon looked beautiful*

Tsurayuki

880   Though I do look

     at it fondly I also

   feel indifferent,

     when I think that its light

     shines upon every garden

Composed when he saw the moon in a pond

881   I never thought

     there could be two, yet now

   a moon rises

     not from the mountain's edge

     but from deep in the water

Accompanying Prince Koretaka[42] on a hunt, they returned to their lodgings, and drank and talked deep into the night, and when the eleven-day moon was about to set, and the Prince, somewhat drunk, was about to retire, he composed

Narihira no Ason

884

Before we get

our fill, why does the moon

set so early?

Move back, O mountain edge,

don't let him get away!

In the reign of the Tamura Sovereign,[43] when Princess Akirakeiko was serving at the Kamo Shrine, there was talk of replacing her due to an offense committed by her mother, and once the charge was dropped, she composed

Nun Kyōshin

885

As it passes

through the great sky, the moon

shines so clearly,

even concealed by clouds

its light cannot be hidden

---

42   A son of Emperor Montoku, he entered the priesthood in 872.
43   Emperor Montoku (r. 850–858).

Topic unknown

Author unknown

889 This is me now,

    but long ago I too

  enjoyed my time

    of glory while I climbed

    up the slopes of Male Mountain

890 There are two things

    that have aged in this world:

  one is the bridge

    of Nagara in Tsu

    and the other is myself

905   If it has been
            so long since I saw it,
        how many reigns
            must have passed for the pine
            on Suminoe beach?

908   And so is this
            how life comes to an end?
        Since I am not
            the pine that stands upon
            the peak of Takasago . . .

On a day when the Dharma Sovereign[44] was visiting the West River,[45] he was commanded to compose on the topic of cranes standing on the bars in the river

Tsurayuki

919 The cranes standing

    in the reeds by the shore,

  resemble waves

    that are drawn by the wind

    but refuse to return

When Prince Nakatsukasa[46] had a boat built for the lake in his mansion, on the day it was lowered into the water and they enjoyed it for the first time, the Dharma Sovereign came to see it. Towards dusk, as they were returning, she composed and presented

Ise

920 If my lord were

    a boat floating upon

  the water then

    I would be sure to say

    that he come here to berth

---

44 A title of Retired Emperor Uda.

45 Another name for the Ōi River. Uda's excursion was in 907.

46 Uda's son Prince Atsuyoshi (888–930).

Composed at a place called Karakoto (Chinese Zither)

Dharma Master Shinsei

921   Karakoto,

    its name resounds as far as

  the capital

    on the strings of the waves

    that are played by the wind

Composed at the Nunohiki waterfalls

Ariwara no Yukihira no Ason

922   Let me gather

    these scattering white pearls

  from the waterfall

    to borrow them as tears

    when my world turns to sadness

In the Reign of the Tamura Sovereign, when he visited the quarters of the ladies-in-waiting to see a folded screen, he was struck by the [scene of a] waterfall cascading and commanded them to compose on this topic

Sanjō no Machi

930   Is this perhaps
       the waterfall of feelings
   from my dammed heart,
     cascading before me
     without making a sound?

Composed on the blossoms in a painting on a folded screen

Tsurayuki

931   From the moment
       they blossomed and thereafter,
   is it because
     their world is spring forever
     their colors do not change?

VOLUME 18—MISCELLANEOUS SONGS 2

Topic unknown

Author unknown

933 What in the world
   remains truly forever?
  yesterday's pools
   in the Asuka River
   today have turned to shallows

934 It is not like
   my body has more than
  one life to live,
   so why do my thoughts scatter
   like seaweed cut by fisherfolk?

Sosei

947
Where will I go
to leave behind the world,
if my feelings
should also go astray
in the fields and the hills?

Author unknown

948
I wonder if
the world has been this hard
since long ago?
Or is it just for me
it is always like this?

A song in which no two letters are the same

Mononobe no Yoshina

955 I would enter

    the mountain path and leave

  all this hardship

    if the person I love

    were not holding me captive

Sent to a mountain dharma master

Ōshikōchi no Mitsune

956 Those who renounce

    the world to enter the mountains

  where do they go,

    when even in the mountains

    there are times they feel miserable?

Composed when he was exiled to the Land of Oki

Takamura no Ason

961   I never thought
             that I would come to this
        here in the wild
             threading a fishing rope
             and angling for a living

In the Tamura era, when he was living due to circumstances[47] in a place called Suma in the land of Tsu, he sent this to someone in the palace.

Ariwara no Yukihira no Ason

962   If someone asks
             what has become of me
        tell them I pine
             just like the salty tides
             that are in Suma bay

[47] In exile.

*When Muneoka no Ōyori came back from Koshi, saw the snow had
piled up and said, "my thoughts of you have accumulated just like this
snow," he composed*

Mitsune

978   Why should I trust
             thoughts that accumulate
       just like the snow?
             once the spring has arrived
             they will all be long gone

Response

Muneoka no Ōyori

979   On the white hills
             of Koshi which I crossed
       thinking of you,
             is there ever a time
             when the snow is all gone?

After conversing with a woman friend, she sent this to her after taking her leave

                                    Michinoku

992   Is it because

                    it dropped into my sleeves

            as we parted

                    that I feel like my spirit

                    is no longer within me?

In the Kanpyō era, when he was appointed aide to the Tang embassy, he was in attendance to the Crown Prince and when each of the men received wine, in turn he composed

                                Fujiwara no Tadafusa

993   With the first frost

                    that follows the long night

            lying upon

                    the soft bamboo I wake

                    in the midst of my thoughts

Topic unknown

Author unknown

994   When the wind blows

　　and at sea waves are rising

Mount Tatsuta

　　is my lord late at night

　　crossing it all alone?

According to a certain person, this song is by a woman who was living long ago with a man in the province of Yamato. Because her parents were deceased and her house's fortunes had dwindled, the man began visiting another woman in Kawachi Province, and gradually his affections drifted away. In spite of this, she never showed resentment and every time he visited Kawachi she encouraged him to go, so the man became suspicious and thought she might be loving another in his absence, and so on a beautiful moonlit night, he pretended to set out for Kawachi but hid instead in the bushes in the garden and watched as late into the night she played the koto while lamenting, and then composed this song before retiring to sleep, and after hearing it, from that time on the man never visited anyone else, or so the story goes.

In the Kanpyō era, presented as his contribution together with other songs

Fujiwara Kachion

999 My heart's feelings,
  which no one else can know,
like the spring haze
  I wish they would rise up
  to appear before my lord

When the sovereign had commanded songs to be presented, at the time of the presentation, she composed this, wrote it at the end of the scroll and presented it

Ise

1000 I only hear
  the mountain river's rumors
from the palace;
  I wish I could return
  and see it once again

VOLUME 19—MISCELLANEOUS FORMS

A long song as a preface to the presentation of old songs to the sovereign

Tsurayuki

1002   Since the age of

the thousand mighty gods

without ceasing

throughout each and every reign

the echoes soar

over Otowa Mountain

while the spring haze

is clouding people's feelings

and summer rains

resound throughout the skies

while night deepens

as the cuckoo in the mountains

with its sad cries

keeps everyone awake

gazing upon

the scarlet leaves just like

Chinese brocade

upon Tatsuta Mountain,

while the autumn rains

fall in the godless month

on winter nights

when the garden is dappled

with falling snow

before it melts away,

thus every year

according to the season

we do express

       our sentiments with words

wishing our lord

       will live one thousand years

while the feelings

       of people in this world

burn just like the

       peak of Fuji in Suruga

parting in tears

       before having their fill

sadly weaving

       lavender robes in mourning;

and each of these

       innumerable words

in accordance

       with our sovereign's commands

in these volumes

       we wanted to include

and as if they

       were seashells on the beach

at Ise bay

       we tried to collect them,

though like gem threads

       we fear to have fallen

short of the task;

       And now the years have passed

as we did serve

       the great palace beneath

the distant skies
     both by day and by night
without question
     or ever looking back
at our own homes
     where the roofs are decayed
and overgrown
     and surely must be leaking
     in these falling spring rains

ECCENTRIC SONGS

Topic unknown

Author unknown

1011   I came to see

            the plum blossoms and yet

        all I can hear

            are the unrelenting cries

            of that blessed bush-warbler

On the sixth of the seventh month, composed on the theme of Tanabata

Fujiwara no Kanesuke

1014   "Perhaps today?"

            he must wonder impatiently,

        waiting for dawn

            robes tied above his shins

            by the heavenly river

Topic unknown

Archbishop Henjō

1016 Maiden flowers
    as they show off their charms
  in the autumn field,
    what a beautiful sight!
    If only for a while . . .

Author unknown

1017 When autumn comes
    and you cover the fields,
  maiden flowers,
    who will refrain from picking you
    and be content to look?

Author unknown

1023   From the pillow
        to the foot I am besieged
by this longing:
        what can I do but sit
        halfway up in my bed?

1024   I have heard that
        there is a way to everything
—even to love:
        so I stand and then sit
        but still I see no way

Ki no Menoto

1028 Like Mount Fuji,
  all I can do is smolder.
If you would burn,
  then burn, you useless smoke
  that gods cannot put out

Komachi

1030 On a moonless
  night as I yearn for him
my thoughts kindle
  flames leaping in my breast
  and my heart is ablaze

Author unknown

1039   I am in love
            but all I hear from them
    is they are not;
            so I will love no longer
            since my love has no point

1041   For not loving
            the one who did love me,
    do I deserve
            that the one whom I love
            loves me not in return?

Ise

1051   I hear the bridge
        of Nagara in Naniwa
    will be rebuilt.
        To what shall I compare
    this body of mine now?

Author unknown

1061   If everyone
        who thought the world was cruel
    jumped off a cliff
        even the deepest valleys
    would quickly become shallow

VOLUME 20

ROYAL SONGS FROM THE GREAT BUREAU OF SONGS

■

A Song for the Great Naobi Deity

1069   And so may we

                        at the very beginning

                of the New Year

                        gather firewood with joy

                to last one thousand years

In the Chronicles of Japan[48] *it says, "and may we serve with joy for a myriad ages"*

Ōmi Style

1070   As I set out

                        in the morning from Ōmi,

                on the Une fields

                        the cranes are crying out

                        as the night draws to an end

[48] This does not actually refer to the *Chronicles of Japan* (*Nihongi*), but to the *Chronicles of Japan Continued* (*Shoku Nihongi*).

DIVINE RITUAL SONGS

An object-holding song

1074   The sakaki leaves

            that grow on the divine

        Mount Mimuro,

            grow all the more profusely

            when in the godly presence

A Sun Goddess Song

1080   Deep in the groves

            of Hinokuma River

        we stop our steeds

            and let them drink a while

            hoping to see the light[49]

[49] A similar poem appears in *Man'yōshū*, vol. 12 (#3097), with a different last measure that makes it a love poem.

1082   The gold we mine
                from Nakayama in Kibi
        circles around
                the slender valley river
                resounding pure and clear

This is a song from the land of Kibi for the Jōwa accession[50]

1084   Land of Mino
                bordered by Fuji River
        which without rest
                will flow to serve our lord
                to last a myriad ages

This is a song from Mino for the Gangyō accession[51]

---

[50]   The accession of Emperor Ninmyō (r. 833–850). The last three measures are
        identical to those of a poem in *Man'yōshū*, vol. 7 (#1102).
[51]   Emperor Yōzei (r. 876–844).

1085   My lord's reign
          we are sure will have no limit
    just like the grains
        of sand at Nagahama
        cannot ever be counted

This is a song from the land of Ise for the Ninna accession[52]

1086   Here in Ōmi,
          the home of Mirror Mountain,
    we have witnessed
        already in its reflection
        our lord's one thousand years

This is a song from Ōmi for the present sovereign's accession[53]

[52] Emperor Kōkō (r. 884–887).
[53] Emperor Daigo (r. 897–930).

SONGS OF THE EAST

Song from Michinoku

1093   Were my heart false
        and I to turn my back
    upon my lord,
        the waves would reach beyond
        the peak of Matsu Mountain

Song from Hitachi

1095   On Mount Tsukuba
        there is shade on one side
    and on the other
        but no shade that surpasses
        the radiance of my lord

A song from the winter Kamo Festival

Fujiwara no Toshiyuki no Ason

1100   The Kamo shrine
              has a thousand mighty gods
         and a young pine
              that in a thousand years
              will never change its colors

KANA PREFACE

THE SONGS OF YAMATO take the human mind[1] as their seed and grow into myriad leaves of words.[2] The people who live in this world, in their abundant concerns and affairs, relate the thoughts in their minds to the things they see and hear, and so express them. Hearing the voices of the bush-warblers that sing among the flowers, of the frogs that live in the water, among all living creatures, what could there be that does not compose songs? It is songs that without using force move heaven and earth, bring compassion to invisible spirits and gods, soften the

---

1   "Mind" translates the word *kokoro* (こころ), which depending on the context, can also be rendered as "heart," "feelings," "meaning," or "intent." Instances of any of these words in this rendition of the Kana Preface all translate the word *kokoro*. This broad use of *kokoro* contrasts with corresponding passages in the Mana Preface that use a variety of different terms such as 心 (mind or heart), 情 (feelings or emotions), and 趣 (intent or import).

2   The opening statement is a conventional pun on *koto no ha* (leaves of things) and *kotoba* ("words").

relations between men and women, and console the hearts of brave warriors.

These songs appeared from the very time that heaven and earth began to open. Yet their transmission to this realm started in the far and distant heavens with Princess Shitateru,[3] and on the ore-rich earth, they began with the god Susa-no-o.[4] In the age of the thousand mighty gods, songs had no defined number of letters,[5] their expression was rustic, and their meaning unclear. Then the age of humans arrived, and since the time of the god Susa-no-o, they have been composed in thirty letters and one.

In this way, such feelings that praise the blossoms, or admire the birds, that are moved by the haze, or are saddened by the dew, have become many and various words. Just as a journey to a distant place begins by setting forth with a single step and then lasts months or years, or just as a high mountain begins as a speck of dust and then grows until it reaches the trailing clouds in heaven, so too has it been with these songs.

3 This refers to two poems in the *Nihon shoki* attributed to the goddess Shitateru-hime.

4 According to the *Nihon shoki*, Susa-no-o, brother of the sun-goddess Amaterasu, was exiled to the earth after causing havoc in heaven. On earth, after various conquests, he arrived in Suga in the land of Izumo, and composed the following poem: "Rising eight clouds / Izumo eightfold fences / to keep my wife / eightfold fences I build / ah yes those eightfold fences." The preface proposes this as the earliest example of a poem composed in five measures and thirty-one syllables, in the pattern 5/7/5/7/7.

5 "Letters" refers to phonographic letters (i.e., *kana*) and thus also to what we call "syllables."

The Naniwazu song was the beginning of the imperial court.[6] The words of Mount Asaka were composed as an amusement by a tribute maiden.[7] These two songs are like the father and mother of song, and have been the first models for those who begin to write.

There are six forms of song. It appears that this is also the case with the songs of Kara.[8] The first of those six types is the suggestive song. This song suggests the Ōsazaki sovereign:[9]

At Naniwa
    flowers bloom on the branches;
winter-hidden,
    now that the spring arrives
    flowers bloom on the branches

6   That is, the first song of the Yamato court. Naniwazu was the palace of the legendary Sovereign Nintoku (traditional reign dates, 313–399). This poem is the example given for the "suggestive song" later in the preface. This poem also appears on wooden slips (*mokkan*) discovered at archaeological sites where it is clear that it was used for writing practice. The oldest of these is estimated to be from Tenmu's reign (672–686), more than two hundred years before the compilation of the *Kokinshū*.

7   See poem 3807 from the *Man'yōshū:* Mount Asaka / whose shadow is reflected / over the pond / which is as shallow / as my love for you is not. Archaeological evidence also suggests that this poem was used as a writing model.

8   Kara refers to the imperial dynasties of China. These "six styles" seem to be equivalents to the "six principles" in the Mana Preface, and in the "Great Preface" to the *Mao* recension of the *Classic of Poetry*. As in the Mana Preface, the purpose of listing these six styles seems to be primarily to declare "Yamato songs" the equal of "songs of Kara."

9   The Ōsazaki sovereign refers to the ruler more commonly known as Nintoku.

The second is the expository song:

> Just how foolish
>> is this body that clings
> to the blossoms,
>> unaware that their beauty
>> causes nothing but pain[10]

The third is the figurative song:

> If you leave me
>> like frost upon the ground
> in the morning,
>> whenever I feel longing
>> will I too melt away?

The fourth is the comparative song:

> All my longing
>> cannot ever be counted
> even less than
>> grains of sand on the beach
>> could possibly be counted

10 The poem has several hidden puns: "This body that clings" (*tuku mi*) can also be read as "thrush" (*tukumi*); "foolish" (*adikinasa*) contains the word *adi* (a type of water bird); "pain" (*itatuki*) also can mean "pierced" and conceals the word "crane (*tatu*). The word to "enter" (*iru*) the body, (translated as to "cause" pain) also means to "take aim." This second form of the song seems to correspond to volume 10 of the *Kokinshū*, "Names of Things," which includes only poems with hidden words.

The fifth is the forthright song:

> If only this
>> were a world without lies,
> then all the words
>> that are spoken by people
>> would bring nothing but joy

The sixth is the panegyric song:

> How wonderful
>> and splendid is this palace!
> Just like clover
>> with three leaves and four leaves
>> its pillars have been built

The world today is attached to colors, and since people's feelings have become like blossoms, all we see are trivial songs and fleeting words: just like trees that are buried in the garden of amorous pleasures and remain unknown, they do not emerge upright like pampas grass in their proper place.[11] If we think of the beginning, it was nothing like this. The sovereigns of the reigns of old, on the flowery mornings of spring or on the moonlit nights of autumn, would send for their attendants and command them to compose songs fit for each occasion. Some, enchanted by the blossoms, would wander in unfamiliar

---

11 The suggestion is that waka, or "the songs of Yamato," have been confined to informal contexts for too long, and should occupy a more central and public position at court.

places; others, yearning for the moon, would follow through the unknown darkness; and the sovereign, gazing into their minds, would discern which of them were wise and which were foolish. And this was not all. They also asked favors of their lord, comparing him to the pebbles or alluding to Mount Tsukuba, and upon receiving favor, they were filled with joy beyond their rank, and with happiness that filled their hearts; they likened their longing to the smoke of Mount Fuji, missed their companions with the sound of the grasshoppers, or thought of aging with the pines of Takasago and Suminoe; they remembered their times long ago on Male Mountain, or sighed for the brief flowering of the maiden flower, and in all of this, they consoled themselves with songs.

Moreover, on spring mornings, they would watch the blossoms scatter, and on autumn evenings, they would listen to the leaves fall. Some would lament the waves and the snow that they saw every year in the mirror's reflection, or would be startled by their own state upon seeing the foam on the water and the dew on the grass. Others would feel sad for lost times and for the splendor of yesterday, and those who had been close would grow distant. Yet others would refer to the waves of Mount Matsu, or would scoop the water of the fields, or would gaze deep in thought at the leaves of the bush-clover in autumn, or would count the beats of the snipe's wings at dawn. And others would speak of grievances as numerous as bamboo stems, or would allude to the Yoshino River when they complained about love. Today, for those who hear that there is no longer smoke over Mount Fuji, or that Nagara Bridge has been rebuilt, it is only in songs that they come to find solace.

Although songs have been transmitted since ancient times, it is only from the reign of Nara[12] that they became widespread. Perhaps this was because in that age the sovereign knew the meaning of song. In that reign, Kakinomoto no Hitomaro, of upper third rank, was the sage of song.[13] This was surely because sovereign and subject were united as one.[14] On autumn evenings, the scarlet leaves that flowed on the Tatsuta River seemed to the sovereign's eyes like brocade, and on spring mornings, the cherry blossoms of Mount Yoshino appeared to Hitomaro's mind as clouds. Furthermore, there was a person called Yamanobe no Akahito. His songs were extraordinary and wonderful. It was difficult for Hitomaro to stand over Akahito, or Akahito beneath Hitomaro.[15]

[12] Nara was the old capital (710–794). Just like the Mana Preface's reference to the "Heizei Son of Heaven," "the reign of Nara" appears to refer broadly to the eighth century as a whole and the time when the *Man'yōshū* was compiled.

[13] Kakinomoto no Hitomaro is the greatest poet of the *Man'yōshū* (*Collection of Myriad Ages*, compiled in the eighth century). His dates are unknown, but he composed poetry in the reigns of Jitō (r. 687–697) and Monmu (r. 697–707) and disappeared from the poetic record before the move of the capital to Nara in 710. It is assumed that Tsurayuki could not seriously have believed that someone so sparsely documented as Hitomaro was really of the upper third rank, and therefore a member of the upper ranks of the nobility. In the Heian period (794–1185), the figure of Hitomaro was semideified, as the "sage" or "saint" of poetry (*uta no hijiri*). A few poems are attributed to Hitomaro in the *Kokinshū*, such as the famous *KKS* 409, but both the diction and the rhythm of these poems indicate that they come from a much later period than Hitomaro.

[14] "This" probably refers to Tsurayuki's (ahistorical) contention that the sovereign responsible for the propagation of waka and the sage of poetry were contemporaries. Tsurayuki explains this coincidence in terms of the harmonious relationship between ruler and subject.

[15] Yamabe no Akahito was a court poet who was active approximately between 720 and 735. He was not, therefore, a contemporary of Hitomaro, but was influenced by Hitomaro's poetry. The sense of Tsurayuki's statement is that Akahito was held in no less esteem than Hitomaro, not that Akahito was the greater of the two.

In addition to these, other excellent people made themselves heard in the reigns numerous as bamboo stems, like strands into a rope entwined appearing unceasingly age after age. And thus the songs from before that time[16] were collected and named the *Man'yōshū (Collection of Myriad Ages)*.

Since then, there have scarcely been one or two people with knowledge of ancient matters and of the meaning of songs. Yet even they have both failures and successes. From that reign until now, more than one hundred years have passed, and there have been ten reigns. There have not been many people who composed songs and knew about the matters and songs of ancient times.

Now, in saying the following, it would be inappropriate to speak of people of high office or rank. Except for these, among the famous people from recent reigns,[17] there is Archbishop Henjō, whose songs achieve a good style, but lack sincerity. They are like looking at a woman painted in a picture that moves our hearts in vain. Ariwara no Narihira has too much feeling but not enough expression. He is like a wilting flower whose fragrance remains. Funya no Yasuhide has skillful words, but his style does not follow the content. He is like a merchant who dresses up in expensive clothes. Monk Kisen of Mount Uji has

---

16 "That time" appears to refer to the time Tsurayuki and his contemporaries thought the *Man'yōshū* was compiled.

17 Tsurayuki comments on six poets who would later become known as the "six poetic immortals" (*rokkasen*). Of these, three (Henjō, Narihira, and Komachi) are well known and well represented in the *Kokinshū*. However, the other three poets (Yasuhide, Kisen, and Kuronushi) are more obscure. Tsurayuki elevates these six figures as examples of waka poets, but at the same time, he critiques their style, suggesting indirectly that the correct style of poetry is that which he and his contemporaries practice.

unclear words, without a defined beginning or end: like looking at the autumn moon when it is obscured by the clouds at dawn. Since we do not hear that he composed many songs, we do not really know what he was like. Ono no Komachi is of the line of Sotōrihime of old.[18] She is very sensitive and lacks strength. She seems like a beautiful woman who is sick. That she lacks strength may be because she is a woman. Ōtomo no Kuronushi has a vulgar style. He is like a man in the hills carrying firewood on his back who stops to rest by the shadow of a flowering tree.

In addition to these people, we hear of other names, numerous like the vines that crawl across the fields, or the leaves that grow lush in the forest, but these only had the idea of songs, and knew nothing of style. Now that our sovereign[19] rules beneath heaven, the four seasons have returned nine times. His great benevolence is like the waves that flow up to the outer reaches of the Eight Islands, the shadow of his great compassion extends luxuriant from the foot of Mount Tsukuba, and in his time free from the thousands of affairs of state, as an example that no matter is left beyond his attention, he does not forget the matters of old, and with the intention of reviving past things, and wishing to examine them himself in order to transmit them to future generations, on the eighteenth day of

---

[18] According to the *Nihon Shoki*, Sotōrihime was a concubine of Sovereign Ingyō (traditional reign dates, 412–453). The comparison with Komachi is probably due to a poem attributed to Sotōrihime in the *Nihon Shoki*: "This is the night / that my lover will come / thus it is shown / distinctly in the patterns / of the spider's web," which suggests the figure of a woman waiting, as do many of Komachi's poems (e.g., see *KKS* 656 and *KKS* 1030).

[19] The sovereign refers to Daigo (r. 897–930).

the fourth month of the fifth year of Engi,[20] he commanded us, the Senior Inner Secretary Ki no Tomonori; the Director of the Palace Library Ki no Tsurayuki; the former Junior Clerk of Kai Province, Ōshikōchi no Mitsune; and the Assistant to the Right Palace Guard, Mibu no Tadamine, to offer old songs that were not included in the *Collection of Myriad Ages*, as well as songs of our own. Among these, we were commanded to choose from songs that are decorated with plum blossoms, that listen to the cuckoo bird, that pick autumn leaves, to those that gaze at the snow,[21] as well as songs that refer to the crane and the turtle[22] when thinking of their lords or congratulating people,[23] that long for their spouses while gazing at the autumn bush-clover or the summer grass,[24] that present paper offerings upon reaching Mount Ōsaka,[25] or even various types of songs that are not included in spring, summer, autumn, or winter.[26] In total, one thousand songs,[27] twenty volumes, and we have named it the *Collection of Ancient and Modern Japanese Songs (Kokinwakashū)*.

[20] The "eighteenth day of the fourth month of the fifth year of Engi" refers to the year 905.

[21] Refers to the seasonal poems in the *Kokinshū*, volumes 1–6.

[22] Both the crane and the turtle are motifs of longevity.

[23] Refers to the "Felicitous Songs" in the *Kokinshū*, volume 7.

[24] Refers to the "Love Songs" in the *Kokinshū*, volumes 11–15.

[25] Refers to the "Farewell Songs" in the *Kokinshū*, volume 8. The "paper offerings" refer to a ritual for safe passage.

[26] Refers to the "Miscellaneous Songs" in the *Kokinshū*, volumes 17 and 18, and perhaps to the other volumes that have not been alluded to.

[27] In fact, the first eighteen volumes have one thousand poems, and all twenty volumes have one thousand one hundred poems.

In this way, the songs that we have selected and collected on this occasion, just like the water that runs at the foot of the mountain, will never cease, and since they have accumulated like grains of sand on the shore, there will be no more rumors that they are like the shallows of Asuka River, and there will be only celebration until the stones become rocks.

These pillow words[28] do not have much fragrance of spring flowers, and though our hollow reputations may last long like the autumn nights, we are afraid of people's criticism, and feel ashamed of the meaning of our songs. Yet even so, like the trailing clouds that rise and sit, like the crying deer that wake and sleep, I, Tsurayuki, and the others were also born in this world, and we feel fortunate to have lived at the time of this achievement.

Hitomaro may be gone, but songs will never end. Though the seasons may pass, things may be lost, and joy and sadness come and go, the letters of these songs will be here. If like the threads of the willow they are unceasing, if like the leaves of the pine they do not scatter, if like the vine they stretch long, if like the tracks of a bird they remain,[29] those who can understand the style of song and the meaning of things, just like when they gaze at the moon in the great sky, will revere the old and desire the new.

---

[28] The text appears to be corrupt, but if the reading is correct, "these pillow words" probably means "these introductory words" (i.e., the preface itself).

[29] A reference to the legend of Cang Jie, a subject of the Yellow Emperor (Huang Di), who in the *Shuowen jiezi* (an etymological dictionary from the Later Han) is said to have invented writing after observing the footprints of a bird.

PART II

ESSAYS

Chapter One

POETRY BEFORE THE HEIAN PERIOD

THE *Collection of Ancient and Modern Japanese Songs* (*Kokin-wakashū* 古今和歌集, early tenth century CE) draws on a long tradition of poetry as the supreme form of imperial culture. This tradition originated with the *Classic of Poetry* (*Shijing* 詩経), by far the most frequently cited text in ancient China,[1] and became institutionalized during the Han dynasty (206 BCE–220 CE) with the emergence of rhapsodic forms of poetry to celebrate (and at times critique) imperial authority. But it is with the development of new written lyric forms after the breakdown of the Han imperial order in the third century CE, that poetry became established as the most exalted register of Literary Sinitic—the standard written language that developed to last throughout the ages to document and envision the complicated history and shifting geography of a transdynastic tradition of empire. In this context, just as the genre of historical writing became essential to defining the imperial state as a transdynastic political entity, literary anthologies also came to play a crucial function in defining successive imperial dynasties as the inhabitants of a common and continuous cultural space. The foremost example of this was the *Literary Selections* (*Wen Xuan* 文選), a vast and comprehensive anthology that collected what its compiler Xiao Tong (501–530 CE) regarded as the finest works of the previous eight centuries: rhapsodies and lyrical poems above all, as well as a wide variety of prose genres that exhibited literary skill.

Medieval Sinitic bibliography organized literate knowledge into four categories: Classics, Histories, Masters, and Collections.[2] The first and most prestigious category included the Six Classics (*Changes, Documents, Poetry, Rites, Music,* and *Springs and Autumns*) and their commentaries, as well as Confucian texts, such as the *Classic of Filial Piety* and the *Analects,* and the "minor learning" of dictionaries, primers, and encyclopedias. Histories covered all forms of historical, genealogical, and geographical documentation and narrative, ranging from official dynastic histories to biographies of notable individuals, to regional gazetteers, and to accounts of strange events that we would now classify as fiction and literature. Masters encompassed all areas and schools of philosophical knowledge as well as a broad array of different kinds of technical expertise that was useful to the state. Finally, Collections referred to poetry collections, both the discrete collections of individual authors, and comprehensive collections, such as the *Wen Xuan* that anthologized the works of the most notable authors of the past. Although this bibliographical scheme lists Collections last, reflecting the notion that literary compositions had neither the prestige of the ancient classics, the all-encompassing descriptive power of historical writing, nor the usefulness of philosophical and technical knowledge, literary writing was also regarded as fundamental insofar as the other categories of writing all made use of literary patterns of rhetoric.

In the Japanese archipelago, scribes were employed by kings since at least the fifth century CE, but for a long time, writing was used only by a small number of specialists for limited purposes. It was not until the late seventh century that the Japanese court was transformed into a fully literate bureaucracy.[3] The widespread adoption of Sinographic writing, together with the books, dictionaries, and encyclopedias that formed the basis of bureaucratic literacy, involved the transference of the extensive repertoire of Sinitic ideals of imperial government and culture that had developed in China over the previous millennium. Among these ideals was the notion that if writing was the basis of imperial administration, the ability to write beautifully—epitomized by poetry—represented the foundation of imperial culture. From at least the early eighth century onward, government officials at the imperial academy in the Japanese court were encouraged to study the *Wen Xuan* alongside classics, histories, technical texts, dictionaries, and classified encyclopedias to acquire the literary skills necessary for government administration. As the most culturally prestigious form of Literary Sinitic, Sinitic poetry became a genre practiced by all other East Asian states that used Sinographic writing, including not just Japan but also continental states such as Silla and Parhae. The ability to compose Sinitic poetry was essential to diplomatic occasions, and from the eighth century onward a significant number of talented officials and highly educated aristocrats at the Japanese court could compose Sinitic poetry and exchange written poems with ambassadors from other lands, even as they depended on speech interpreters to converse with them.

Like their counterparts at the Tang court, Japanese officials who wrote Sinitic poetry had learned to read and write by studying books such as the *Analects* and dictionaries such as the *Thousand Graph Text*. They too studied the Classics and their commentaries and also were familiar with Sinitic dynastic histories and philosophical texts. As had been the case in China, the writers of Japanese legal codes and official histories often were talented practitioners of Sinitic poetry. They embodied the celebrated statement by Cao Pi (187–226 CE), the first emperor of the Wei dynasty (220–266 CE) in China, that "literary composition is the great task of governing the state," inasmuch as their literary skills served to document the words and deeds of the sovereign, articulate the laws that gave shape to the state, and celebrate the majesty of the imperial court.[4]

Although Sinitic poetry could serve as an emblem of both governmental expertise and cosmopolitan courtliness, it had no connection to the cultural past of an early Japanese state that had only recently been transformed into a fully literate bureaucracy. The adoption of writing at the Yamato court thus led to the development of a different genre of poetry based on a vernacular tradition, one that featured the local landscape as its geographical setting, and its own royal lineages as the main protagonists. This poetry was called "song" (*uta* 歌) to distinguish it from the cosmopolitan Sinitic genres of "poems and rhapsodies" (*shifu* 詩賦). Unlike Sinitic poetry, which could be vocalized in different languages, Yamato songs could be read as poetry only in the eighth-century Japanese court vernacular.

There has been an unfortunate tendency in scholarship on ancient Japan to think of the contrast between Yamato songs and Sinitic poetry as being primarily a question of linguistic difference, of "poetry written in the Japanese language" versus "poetry written in the Chinese language." This view is based on a fundamental misconception of how writing functioned in medieval East Asia. The primary distinction between Yamato songs and Sinitic poems was not one between different spoken languages but one between different written registers. All Sinographic writing was "Chinese" insofar as the Sinoscript—the writing system of so-called Chinese characters—originated in China and throughout premodern times was associated with the cultural authority of the Chinese imperial dynasties. At the same time, because it developed as a primarily logographic script, it was adopted and became the written language of numerous other states in East Asia and came to be used as a cosmopolitan written form of interstate communication. The classical written style of the Sinoscript—what we refer to as Classical Chinese or Literary Sinitic—was a standard written register designed not only to bridge the local spoken languages of different geographical areas but also to outlast the spoken languages of any specific period and endure throughout the ages. This meant that texts written in orthodox Literary Sinitic could be read by speakers of different languages—including non-Sinitic languages such as Japanese—and therefore were not exclusively associated with any form of spoken Chinese.

For instance, Xiao Tong, the compiler of *Wen Xuan*, spoke a very different form of Chinese language than the followers of Confucius who wrote down the *Analects*. What made it possible for him to read the *Analects* was his participation in the millenarian tradition of exegesis of classical Sinitic texts. This was not too different from how a Japanese court official did not need to speak Chinese to understand the *Analects*, or indeed a poem from the *Wen Xuan*. They learned to read these and other texts in Literary Sinitic through a practice known as "reading by gloss" (*kundoku*). This practice relied on the development of an established lexicon of equivalences between sinographs and Japanese words, conventional ways of transposing them into Japanese word order, and the addition of necessary grammatical elements to form Japanese phrases and sentences.[5] This glossing technique, which probably developed on the Korean Peninsula, allowed aristocrats in Japan and in other non-Sinitic states to gain access to the tradition of literate knowledge that had developed over the preceding millennium in China.

This same glossing system allowed Japanese court officials to write their own texts in Literary Sinitic without learning to speak in Chinese. A good example of this is the *Nihon shoki* (日本書紀 *Chronicles of Japan*, 720 CE), the earliest extant official history of the Japanese court. The *Nihon shoki* blends Sinitic notions of universal sovereignty with local mythologies of kingship to describe Japan as an imperial realm ruled by a lineage of heavenly sanctioned sovereigns with divine ancestors. The *Nihon shoki* is often mischaracterized as being "written in Chinese," but a more accurate description would be that the logographic style of the *Nihon shoki* is quite close to the orthodox Literary Sinitic style of the histories that were written at the Tang court in China, and therefore, it could (and can) indeed be read by a competent reader of Literary Sinitic.[6] But because Sinographic writing in general and the orthodox style of Literary Sinitic in particular could be adapted to different languages, the *Nihon shoki* can also be read by gloss (i.e., vocalized into a form of vernacular Japanese), which in fact is the primary way that the text was read in Japan.

At the same time, the adoption of Sinographic writing also involved the development of new written registers that departed from orthodox Literary Sinitic and were influenced and shaped by the spoken vernaculars of those who wrote them. An example of this is the written style of the *Kojiki* (古事記 *Records of Matters of Antiquity*, 712 CE), another early mytho-historical text that has been described as an experimental style of writing in Japanese. A more accurate and precise formulation would be that the logographic text of the *Kojiki* departs significantly from orthodox Literary Sinitic, to the point that it can be deciphered only with difficulty by a reader of Literary Sinitic who has no knowledge of classical Japanese, and its intended audience is clearly limited to people fluent in the eighth-century Japanese court vernacular. To put it another way, the *Kojiki* was a logographic text written for a local readership, whereas the *Nihon shoki*, in addition to being read in the Japanese court vernacular, could be read by anyone who could read Literary Sinitic, whether they knew Japanese or not.

Understanding these kinds of possible relationships between Sinographic writing and spoken language is crucial to make sense of what vernacular poetry was and how it developed in

Japan. It is unclear when exactly Yamato song first developed as a written genre, that is to say, as a genre in which writing did not function simply as a technology to transcribe an oral performance, nor merely as a script for oral recitation, but rather as a medium in which the poem was intended to be appreciated. Archaeological and textual evidence suggests that this happened in the middle of the seventh century, at around the same time as the court was undergoing its literate revolution. In the initial stages when societies start to become literate, writing often functions to facilitate and complement, rather than replace, existing oral technologies of recording and preserving cultural memory. Indeed, one of the key early functions of writing in many societies is to further enhance prestige forms of oral language through formalization and standardization.[7] It is likely that, in its initial stages, the writing of songs functioned primarily to aid their oral memorization and transmission.

The oldest examples of *uta* appear in the *Kojiki* and *Nihon shoki*. Each text includes more than one hundred songs, about half of which appear in both, either verbatim or in variant form. In both texts, songs are inscribed phonographically, that is, in Sinographs whose Sinitic pronunciation functions to represent the sound of Japanese syllables. This phonographic function was not a unique Japanese development. Although the Sinoscript is primarily a logographic writing system, it features intrinsic phonographic aspects that fulfill essential supplementary functions. For instance, phonographic borrowing was a common way in which new graphs were formed.[8] It was also central to the pedagogy and study of Literary Sinitic writing, as it was necessary to gloss the pronunciation of unknown graphs. A third key function of the phonographic use of graphs was to represent words from non-Sinitic languages whose indigenous pronunciation was regarded as significant, such as personal names and place names. Numerous examples of such use of phonographs appear in Sinitic dynastic histories for the names of rulers and places in neighboring kingdoms.[9] This phonographic function is employed in exactly the same way in texts that were written in Japan, such as the *Kojiki* and *Nihon shoki*, which use phonographs abundantly for personal names, as well as in intra-linear glosses to indicate the indigenous pronunciation of the logographs used to write place names. It is important to distinguish, however, between the use of phonographs to supplement logographic inscription and a case in which the phonographic writing constitutes the main text. The phonographic inscription of the songs in the *Kojiki* and *Nihon shoki* functions to explicitly distinguish them from the surrounding logographic prose writing and thus set them apart as self-contained vernacular texts. This use of phonographic inscription had an important precedent in the treatment of Buddhist dharani or mantras, which unlike other Buddhist texts were written phonographically because their original Sanskrit sounds held special significance. The primary purpose of the phonographic inscription of songs in *Kojiki* and *Nihon shoki* was to represent verbatim versions of the prosodically stylized speeches of the ancestors of the imperial court so that they could be recalled and recited in the present and throughout the ages.[10]

Broadly speaking, the songs of the *Kojiki* and *Nihon shoki* can be categorized into two types according to their formal characteristics: those that adhere to the standard five-measure *tanka* (short song) form in a 5/7/5/7/7 syllabic pattern, and longer songs with an indeterminate number of measures and no discernible syllabic patterns. It is unclear when Yamato song developed its fixed pattern of alternating measures of five and seven syllables, or when the tanka form became established. It is likely that the metric pattern was formed through the influence of phonographic inscription, but this occurred at a stage when writing was still used primarily to facilitate oral performances and recitation. The songs with irregular metrical patterns are believed to be the result of the transcribing and scripting of oral performances of songs about ancient kings. Some songs exhibit a mix of both irregular syllabic patterns and regular 5/7 syllable measures. This mix suggests that they are composites of songs dating from different periods, although some irregular syllabic patterns may be the result of conscious design.

In both the *Nihon shoki* and the *Kojiki*, songs appear from the mythical age of the gods through the reigns of legendary rulers and up to the seventh century. These songs are attributed to the main protagonists of the myth-historical record: the divine ancestors of the imperial house and its successive sovereigns, their wives, and their ministers. Songs in the regular 5/7/5/7/7 tanka form appear from the age of the gods (the first example in both texts is a song attributed to the god Susano-o) up to the seventh century, whereas songs with irregular or undefined meter tend to appear in the older periods. This means that, on the one hand, the modern (i.e., seventh century) five-measure 5/7/5/7/7 form was projected into the legendary and mythical past, while on the other, purportedly ancient song performances could be summoned through the act of reading into the literary present of the eighth-century court. In this way, songs played a key function in the textual creation of an imperial lineage that traced its legitimacy through the centuries to a mythical divine age by providing it with a cultural memory that could be reactivated through reading and recitation. Conversely, the tradition of vernacular song was furnished with a mythical pedigree through its association with the narrative of the imperial lineage.

Most of the extant songs from the seventh and eighth centuries are collected in the *Man'yōshū* (万葉集 *Collection of Myriad Ages*, late eighth century), a vast anthology of more than four thousand five hundred poems that was compiled in several stages throughout the eighth century. Unlike the *Kojiki* and *Nihon shoki*, in which songs are presented as spoken or sung by the protagonists of the historical record, the *Man'yōshū* describes songs as artifacts that have been "composed." With a few exceptions, *Man'yōshū* poems generally follow regular syllabic phrase patterns, the vast majority in the five-measure tanka form of 5/7/5/7/7, with some two hundred and sixty *chōka* or "long songs" of alternating 5/7 measures.[11] In contrast to the strictly phonographic notation of songs in the *Kojiki* and *Nihon shoki*, in the *Man'yōshū*, different volumes adopt a style of inscription that is either primarily logographic (in volumes 1–4, 6, 7–13, and 16) or phonographic (in volumes 5, 14, 15, and 18–20). The only exception is found in volume 17, which includes poems written in both styles. The logographic writing of poetry usually relies on the use of supplementary phonographs to represent various parts of speech such as auxiliary verbs and some particles. In contrast, phonographic inscription usually is entirely phonographic, but it occasionally can include words inscribed logographically for emphasis or stylistic considerations. In theory, logographic inscription emphasizes the connection to the tradition of Sinitic poetry, whereas phonographic inscription rejects (again, in theory) this connection to highlight the vernacular language of the poem. In practice, however, both styles of inscription represent a tradition of vernacular song as *written* poetry insofar as they remain open to considerable expressive variations, including puns and allusions that derive from the interplay between logographic and phonographic writing.[12]

Like the *Wen Xuan*, the *Man'yōshū* is a comprehensive anthology of selected works of the past. Its title "Myriad Ages" strongly suggests aspirations to political and cultural longevity in the future. Because it was compiled in various stages, the *Man'yōshū* makes use of an eclectic variety of organizational principles—historical, geographical, topical, generic—but at the same time displays a pervasive commitment throughout its twenty volumes to configuring the anthology as a universal realm of poetic expression centered on the figure of the imperial sovereign.

The *Man'yōshū* has a reputation for including a broader social range of poets than later waka anthologies. To some extent this is true, even if, as Shinada Yoshikazu has shown, the image of the anthology as a "folk" collection that includes poets from all levels of society is a modern nationalist distortion.[13] The older poems in the first two volumes of the *Man'yōshū* are attributed to sovereigns and (in the case of male sovereigns) to their wives. They are the exemplary authors of poetry and the source of waka's cultural authority. At the same time, lower-ranking poets who are completely absent from the historical record, such as Kakinomoto no Hitomaro, are also important authorial figures in the *Man'yōshū* insofar as they represent poetry as a literary practice that defined the cultural identity of the lower-ranking court officialdom. Substantial archaeological evidence shows court scribes practicing their writing of vernacular poems on wooden tablets, together with phrases from Sinitic texts used for elementary literacy, such as the *Thousand Graph Text* (*Senjimon*) and the *Analects* (*Rongo*). Most of the poems found on wooden tablets dating from the late seventh and eighth centuries are in fact fragments of the same poem, the so-called Naniwazu song, which is mentioned in the kana preface to the *Kokinshū* as a calligraphic model. It is unclear how proficient an average lower-ranking scribe might have been at writing poetry—many of them may not have got much further than the repeated writing of the Naniwazu song. The commonplace inscription of poems on wooden tablets suggests a widespread institutional effort from the late seventh century onward to establish the rhythm and pattern of the 5/7/5/7/7 tanka form of vernacular poetry as a fundamental requirement of courtier literacy that would create a shared sense of cultural belonging. It is evident from the *Man'yōshū* that most midranking officials would have been able to compose a credible tanka poem, but there are also signs of attempts to instill elementary poetic skills in officials of a less privileged status, as attested by poems attributed to frontier soldiers. Such poetic skills, even if limited, conferred a sense of membership in a cultural community centered on the imperial court and of emotional investment in its historical past and political continuity.

The earliest known instance of the term waka, or "Japanese song," to describe this emerging tradition of vernacular poetry is found in volume 5 of the *Man'yōshū*,[14] which is also the earliest volume to employ primarily phonographic notation. The representation of waka as a self-consciously vernacular poetic style of the Japanese imperial court and its comparison and contrast with the cosmopolitan style of Sinitic poetry is also a theme in the work of Ōtomo no Yakamochi (718–785), who is believed to have been the final compiler of the *Man'yōshū*. By the time of the last dated poem in the *Man'yōshū* (759), waka poetry had become established as the preeminent vernacular literary form of the Japanese imperial court. On the one hand, it existed in a continuum with Sinitic poetry and frequently relied upon Sinitic sources. On the other, it also represented an ostensibly independent vernacular poetic realm in Japan, a community of feeling and cultural memory within which the court and its individual members could recognize and define themselves in relation to their local history and geography. As the monumental text of this vernacular poetic realm, the *Man'yōshū* would become the main historical precedent for the renewal of waka poetic tradition in the late ninth century that culminated in the compilation of the *Kokinshū*.

NOTES

1. See Martin Kern, "The Formation of the Classic of Poetry," in *The Homeric Epics and the Chinese Book of Songs: Foundational Texts Compared*, ed. Fritz-Heiner Mutschler (Cambridge: Cambridge Scholars, 2018), 39–71.

2. See Wai-Yee Li's "Editor's Introduction" to "Traditional Genre Spectrum," in *The Oxford Handbook of Classical Chinese Literature (1000 BCE–900 CE)* (New York: Oxford University Press, 2017), 163–169.

3. See David Lurie, *Realms of Literacy: Early Japan and the History of Writing* (Cambridge, MA: Harvard University Asia Center, 2011), especially "A World Dense with Writing: Expanding Literacies in the Seventh and Eighth Centuries," 115–166.

4. See *Monzen (Wen Xuan): Bunshōhen, ge*, 199.

5. This definition is a paraphrase of Lurie, *Realms of Literacy*, 179.

6. The scholarly consensus is that the *Nihon shoki* was probably written by two different scribes, one of whom was probably a native speaker of Chinese (perhaps a Tang native) and another who was a native speaker of Japanese. See Mori Hiromichi, *Nihon shoki no nazo o toku: Jussakusha wa dare ka* (Tokyo: Chūko Shinsho, 1999).

7. See, for instance, Saitō Mareshi's discussion of writing in early China in *Kanji sekai no chihei: Watashitachi ni totte moji to wa nanika* (Tokyo: Shinchō sensho, 2014). See also Gregory Nagy's discussion of ancient Greece in *Homeric Questions* (Austin: University of Texas Press, 1996).

8. A commonly cited example of this is the formation of 我, the graph for the personal pronoun "I." Originally the meaning of "I" was represented by the borrowed usage of the homophone graph for spear (戈), and it was eventually distinguished by the later addition of the graph radical for hand (手) on its left side. Known as "provisional borrowing" (仮借, J. *kasha*, or C. *jiajie*), this is one of six types of graph formation outlined by Han dynasty historian Ban Gu, in the "Treatise on Arts and Letters" volume of the *Book of Han*.

9. A famous example of this is the name Himiko (卑弥呼, the She-King of the Wa People) described in the "Eastern Barbarians," in *Records of Three Kingdoms (Sanguozhi*, ca. 297 CE).

10. The difference between the logographic prose text and the phonographic poems is, once again, not a question of linguistic difference. Instead, it is the difference between a vernacular "reading by gloss" of the prose text, which allows for some variation while adhering to the basic meaning of the written text, and the verbatim recitation of the sounds of the text, in which case the reciter or reader may not be familiar with the meaning of all of the words. Note the important difference between the phonographic notation of songs in the *Kojiki* and the *Nihon shoki*: Whereas the phonographic inscription of the *Kojiki* songs employs commonly used

phonographs, the *Nihon shoki* songs are written in phonographs that seem to have been deliberately selected for their obscurity or complexity. Reading the *Nihon shoki* poems thus would have required a higher level of literacy (as would reading the *Nihon shoki* itself).

11. There are also sixty-odd examples of a six-measure variant of the *tanka* called *sedōka*, in a pattern of 5/7/7/5/7/7, and a single example of another variant form known as the Buddha Stone Footprint poem, *bussokusekika*, in the pattern 5/7/5/7/7/7.

12. For a more detailed account of the various styles of inscription in the *Man'yōshū*, see "The Poetry of Writing," in Lurie, *Realms of Literacy*, 255–311.

13. Shinada Yoshikazu, "*Man'yōshū*: The Invention of a National Poetry Anthology," in *Inventing the Classics: Modernity, National Identity, and Japanese Literature* (Stanford, CA: Stanford University Press, 2002), 31–50.

14. From the Heian period onward, the word waka was usually written as 和歌. In the *Man'yōshū*, this term is used to mean "a poem in response" (and is given the vernacular reading of *kotafuru uta*), whereas waka in the sense of Japanese poetry is written as 倭歌, with the earlier graph 倭 for Japan. Even after the adoption of the graph 和 to mean Japan in the eighth century, both graphs continued to be used interchangeably until the mid-Heian period, as attested to by the fact that the earliest extant manuscript of the *Kokinshū* uses the graph 倭歌 in its title.

Chapter Two

THE HEIAN COURT AND KANA WRITING

THE TEMPORAL DISTANCE between the compilation of the *Man'yōshū* in the late eighth century and that of the *Kokinshū* in the early tenth century appears further amplified by the momentous political and cultural changes that occurred during this period. First among these was the move of the capital from Nara to Heian, and the subsequent reconfiguration of the imperial administration and court culture around this new geographical locale. Second was the development of cursive kana script, which became the standard medium in which to write waka after the tenth century. These changes transformed waka poetry to such an extent that the poetry of the *Man'yōshū* and the Nara period quickly came to be perceived as belonging to an archaic age.

Emperor Kanmu (r. 781–806), who moved the capital first to Nagaoka in 784 and then to Heian in 795, portrayed his reign as the inauguration of a new dynastic branch of the imperial line.[1] Placing a renewed emphasis on Confucian ideals of kingly rule and on the reform of Buddhist institutions, Kanmu also sought to expand the frontiers of the realm with military campaigns against the Emishi peoples in Northeastern Japan. The reigns of his three sons, Heizei (r. 806–09), Saga (r. 809–23), and Junna (r. 823–33), were marked by a reinvigorating infusion of new forms of cultural knowledge and technologies brought back by an embassy to the Tang court in 804–805. Foremost among these were the transmission of the Tendai and Shingon schools of Buddhism by the monks Saichō (767–822) and Kūkai (774–835), which led to the establishment of new Buddhist centers in and around the Heian capital. Other reforms during this period included the institutionalization of Sinitic forms of court ritual as well as the establishment of scholarly lineages to staff the imperial university.

The transmission of the latest Tang styles of Sinitic literary thought, poetry, and calligraphy to the Japanese court also led to a golden age for the practice of Sinitic poetry, as illustrated by the official compilation of three consecutive imperial anthologies in the early ninth century. Like their Nara-period predecessor the *Kaifūsō*, the first two were relatively small collections: *Ryōunshū* (*The Cloud Soaring Collection*, 814) included only ninety-two poems in a single volume, and *Bunka Shūreishū* (*Collection of Literary Masterpieces*, 818) consisted of one hundred and forty-eight poems in three volumes. Both of these were the work of a small community of less than thirty authors, including the emperor (Saga), his ministers, and scholars of the imperial university. The third anthology, *Keikokushū* (*Collection for Governing the State*, 827), was much larger, comprising twenty volumes (of which only six are extant) with more than nine hundred poems and around ninety compositions of literary prose, by one hundred and seventy-eight different authors, and was clearly modeled on the *Wen Xuan*. The emperors (Saga and Junna), ministers, and scholars who compiled these anthologies did not look back to their Nara-period predecessors as exemplars. For instance, none of the prefaces to the collections mention the *Kaifūsō*, in spite of its close association with Tenchi (r. 661–672), the imperial ancestor of the Heian sovereigns. Rather, they modeled themselves on the court of Emperor Cao Pi of the Wei Dynasty in China, whose adage "literary composition is the great task of governing the state" features prominently in the preface to *Bunka shūreishū* and in the title *Keikokushū* (*Collection for Governing the State*).[2] They saw themselves as latter-day Japanese equivalents of Cao Pi's poetic circle during the Jian'an era (196–220 CE),[3] as the inaugurators of a new age and a new capital city whose rulers and officials' fluency in the cosmopolitan Sinitic tradition of literary and administrative knowledge aspired to emulate the Tang court.

This golden age of Sinitic poetry at the early Heian court is often characterized as the "dark age" of waka. Notably, however, throughout the ninth century, the practice of vernacular song at court continued to play an important role in the cultural logic of imperial accession. The practice of Sinitic poetry may have enabled Heian courtiers to represent themselves as cosmopolitan inheritors of the Sinitic cultural tradition, but only waka poetry could function as a marker of cultural continuity for the imperial lineage. Indeed, most of the few waka poems recorded in the official histories during this period either celebrate or foretell the accession of a new emperor.

Throughout this period, waka in the five-measure tanka form were written phonographically, whereas long poems were written in a mixed style that supplemented logographs with phonographs for particles and inflected parts of speech, similar to the style of writing imperial edicts (*senmyō*) in official histories. In fact, phonographic writing in full-form standard sinographs continued to be used in formal contexts for the rest of the ninth century and into the first half of the tenth century, as confirmed by waka recorded in *Ruijū kokushi*, a historical encyclopedia compiled in 892, and in the *Nihongi* lecture banquets of the late-ninth to mid-tenth century.[4] At the same time, simplified forms of phonographic writing gradually developed into the distinct phonographic scripts that came to be known as *kana*, an invention that was probably inspired by the example of the Sanskrit Siddham script.

The etymology and meaning of the term *kana* is somewhat ambiguous.[5] There is consensus that it derives from the term *karina* (via the contraction *kanna*), but it is unclear whether *karina* originally meant "borrowed graphs" or "provisional graphs" (its logographic writing as 仮名 or 仮字 can suggest either or both senses). In the former sense, the term *kana* refers to the function of the script—that is, to the borrowing of the sound of sinographs to write phonographically. According to this definition, the phonographic use of sinographs in the *Kojiki* and *Nihon shoki* or in the *Man'yōshū* can be regarded as a form of kana writing), as it is in the use of the much-later terms *Man'yōgana* (万葉仮名) or *magana* (真仮名),[6] and the Heian kana scripts merely represent simplified stylistic developments of phonographic writing. In the latter sense, however, the meaning of *kana* as "provisional graphs" describes the cursivized or abbreviated *shape* of kana graphs. It is this sense that forms a contrast with the term *mana* (真名 or 真字), which often is incorrectly translated as "true" graphs, but actually refers to "full-form" or "standard" sinographs in contrast to the "shorthand" kana script.[7] The term *mana* is also used in a variety of senses in different contexts to refer to writing that is formal in the following ways: it refers to sinographs as opposed to kana script and therefore by implication to Literary Sinitic in contrast to kana vernacular writing, and is also used to distinguish the phonographic use of full-form Sinographs from kana script, as well as to differentiate standard sinographic script (*shinsho* 真書 or *seisho* 正書), from "running" or semicursive script (*gyōsho* 行書), and "draft" or cursive script (*sōsho* 草書).[8]

The two different styles of kana script developed in distinct contexts.[9] The script known as katakana derived from sets of abbreviated phonographs used to write interlinear glosses and intralinear notes in documents written in various registers of Literary Sinitic, most notably, Buddhist texts. Katakana symbols developed in various ways from both standard-style phonographs and cursive forms, primarily through a process of abbreviation as well as with some significant cursivization. Katakana developed as an eminently practical script, designed for easy recognition even at a small size, to function almost exclusively as a supplement to sinographic writing. Cursive kana, the style that would later be called *hiragana*[10] but in the Heian period was referred to simply as *kana*, developed through the further cursivization of phonographs written in *sōsho*, the informal yet refined cursive style used for unofficial or personal writings in Literary Sinitic.

In China, the earliest forms of cursive writing developed from the clerical script (*reisho* 隷書) used for bureaucratic writing during the Han dynasty as a way of increasing writing speed.[11] With the increasingly widespread availability of paper, the development of brush-making technology, and the emergence of expressive literary writing as a bibliographical category, more refined styles of semicursive and cursive writing developed among cultural elites in the third and fourth centuries CE. A key element in the creation of a shared calligraphic tradition was the canonization of Wang Xizhi (303–361 CE) as the "sage of calligraphy" and the adoption of his transmitted works as writing models throughout Buddhist institutions during the Sui dynasty, and subsequently at the court of the second Tang emperor, Taizong (r. 626–642). Wang's semicursive style had a profound influence on the development of both a more stylish form of standard script that replaced the old Han dynasty clerical script and on the emergence of cursive calligraphy as an artistic genre.[12] By the Tang dynasty, a sociocultural space set apart from the business of official administrative writing and defined by the practice of the so-called three perfections—the leisurely arts of poetry, calligraphy, and painting—had become an essential aspect of a civilized courtly identity.[13] Cursive and semicursive scripts thus came to function as calligraphic registers for belletristic writing, including not only poetry and literary essays but also genres with more practical social and religious functions, such as personal letters, funerary elegies, or Buddhist prayers. Because cursive writing allowed for a far greater range of expressive variation than standard script, talented calligraphers could develop distinctive and recognizably personal styles of handwriting. Two notable examples of this are the Tang court official Zhang Xu (fl. eighth century CE) and his younger contemporary the Buddhist monk Huaisu (737?–785? CE), who developed styles of linked cursive writing in which entire sequences of Sinographs were written without lifting the brush from the paper.[14] It was these styles of linked cursive Sinographic writing that were the continental precedents of the linked cursive kana script.

The earliest extant instances of cursive calligraphy in Japan date from the early Heian period and are attributed to Kūkai and Emperor Saga. Unlike standard script or the more circumscribed forms of semicursive script that characterized the work of professional scribes, the artistic forms of cursive calligraphy that developed in the early Tang were ostentatious and deliberately extravagant (even if such extravagance could be conventionalized) and allowed for the expression of a personal style that could be admired and recognized by those fellow literati familiar with the writer's hand. Cursive writing could be practical, but at a certain level, it was regarded as masterful. Although it was "informal," when practiced by a talented calligrapher, it became a virtuoso form of written performance that represented the calligraphic personality and cultural authority of the writer and constituted an object worthy of display and preservation. Cursive writing also played a significant role in ideals of male friendship among elites, whereby the "knowing" of another's handwriting signified being in touch with their thoughts and feelings.[15] Several of the extant examples of early-ninth-century Heian cursive calligraphy are documents that memorialize such friendships, such as the correspondence between Kūkai and Saichō, or

Saga's elegiac poem on Saichō's death. Although characterized as "informal" or "personal" documents, the very fact that they survive means they also were objects intended for display and for preservation as historical testaments of the personal bonds between powerful men of letters at the Heian court.

With the exception of some late-ninth-century fragmentary inscriptions on manuscripts and pottery, the *Kokinshū* is the earliest extant text that features waka written in cursive kana. It is likely that the writing of the *Kokinshū* represents the culmination of a practice that emerged sometime in the middle of the ninth century among the literary elite of writing waka in cursive phonographs rather than in standard or semicursive script. Given what we know about the social function of waka as a form of literary correspondence, it is likely that cursive kana developed from the use of cursive Sinographic script (*sōsho*) in personal letters. The history of waka as a form of epistolary writing goes back to the *Man'yōshū*, which features several examples of literary correspondence between male courtiers, particularly those in the Ōtomo lineage, such as the main compiler Yakamochi and his father Tabito, who emulate Sinitic poetry exchanges between men anthologized in the *Wen Xuan* and other collections.[16] However, the vast majority of epistolary waka poetry consists of amorous exchanges between men and women. The *Man'yōshū* genre of *sōmon* (a term that means "exchanges" and is used in the sense of "written correspondence" in the *Wen Xuan*), is mostly made up of amorous poetry. Moreover, the genre of poetic correspondence between lovers is provided with a mythical origin in the *Nihon shoki* tale of the heavenly god Hiko hoho-demi's exchange with Toyotamahime, the daughter of the sea god, as is explicitly acknowledged in the Mana Preface to the *Kokinshū*. Both waka poetry and cursive kana, therefore, were closely associated with an amorous register of literary expression.

As Komatsu Hideo has argued, the development of linked cursive kana, that is to say, the writing of sequences of kana graphs without lifting the brush, had the highly functional result of making it possible to group syntactical phrases into graphic units and thus render intelligible the phonographic writing of Japanese vernacular prose.[17] This, in turn, made it possible to frame waka poems in vernacular prose contexts and thus for a written prose vernacular to develop around waka. In this respect, it is important to emphasize that the *Kokinshū* was, in addition to being the earliest anthology of cursive kana poetry, also the first to write its prose paratexts—the headnotes and endnotes that accompany the poems—in cursive kana.[18] The compilation of the *Kokinshū* thus marked the conscious establishment of cursive kana as a written register for vernacular poetry and related prose writings.[19]

Standard descriptions of this written register often emphasize that cursive kana was a gendered form of writing. Such accounts tend to be structured by a series of binary oppositions: mana writing is often described as being "in Chinese," the exclusive domain of male court officials, and reserved for official "public" documents. Conversely, the kana script is described as being "in Japanese" and belonged to the "private" sphere accessible to female aristocrats. This framework of binary oppositions has many problems. First, the contrast between mana and kana is not between different spoken languages but rather between different registers of writing: when the term mana refers to Literary Sinitic writing, it can be vocalized in "Chinese" or in "Japanese."[20] The notion of a contrast between "public" writing that is gendered male and "private" writing that is gendered female does have some validity, but it is more complex and nuanced than a simple binary opposition.

Note that the kana/mana distinction, together with its gendered aspects, initially was limited to and the product of kana prose discourse, because it was kana that needed to be defined as a written register vis-à-vis the orthodox form of mana. The gendering of cursive kana as "women's writing" and its contrast with "men's writing" appears to have existed since at least the early tenth century and probably since the development of cursive kana writing. In the *Tosa Diary* (ca. 935), the main compiler of the *Kokinshū*, Ki no Tsurayuki (872?–945?), uses both the term "female graphs" (*womunamoji*) to refer to cursive kana writing and "male graphs" (*wotokomoji*) to refer to Sinographic writing in Literary Sinitic.[21] Cursive kana is also referred to with some frequency as "women's hand" (*wonnade*) in mid-Heian vernacular texts. The existence of numerous diaries and tales in cursive kana script attributed to women from the mid-Heian period onward has led to a misconception that terms such as *wonnade* meant "writing *by* women." In fact, judging by the context in which it appears, *wonnade* appears to have referred to a distinct linked cursive kana style that originally was distinguished from a nonlinked cursive form of phonographic writing called "men's hand" (*wotokode*), which was a far less common term of which there are only two extant examples.[22] This strongly suggests that the meaning of *wonnade* is something more akin to "feminine writing." In its earliest examples in mid-Heian texts, such as *The Tale of the Hollow Tree* (*Utsuho monogatari*, ca. 970), *The Kagerō Diary* (*Kagerō nikki*, ca. 974), *The Pillow Book* (*Makura no sōshi*, ca. 996), or *The Tale of Genji* (*Genji monogatari*, ca. 1008), *wonnade* seems to have been used to describe not who was writing, but rather those for whom the writing was intended or suited. A similar qualification applies to the single instance of the term *wonnabumi* (woman's letter), which appears in a famous section in the "Broom Tree" chapter of the *Tale of Genji* about a scholar's daughter who makes too frequent use of *mana* in a "woman's letter" (i.e., in cursive kana correspondence).[23] From these texts, it is abundantly clear that (1) men wrote in cursive kana or "women's hand" when they wrote to women, (2) women used mana on occasion in their correspondence with men (and also when ghost-writing for men), and (3) men could write in kana to other men when they wanted to communicate in a certain kind of informal register or when the letter was also going to be read by a woman.[24]

The idea that cursive kana was called *wonnade* because it was used primarily by women is also related to the misconception that women did not learn to write Sinographs or Literary Sinitic.[25] Although Sinographic writing was associated primarily with male court officials, a famous passage describing models for writing practice in the *Tale of the Hollow Tree* suggests that, even as late as the mid-Heian period, aristocratic women had to first practice Sinographic calligraphy before learning how to write proper cursive kana.[26] It is also clear that many male officials were not particularly skilled at Sinographic writing and that while it may have been unseemly or socially inappropriate for women to write mana *as themselves*, some highly literate women "ghost-wrote" in Literary Sinitic for their male relatives (or for their lovers—as is the case in the story about the scholar's daughter in the "Broom Tree"). A more nuanced and precise description of cursive kana, therefore, is that it was an informal style of writing associated with unofficial social spaces in and around the court that were more accessible to aristocratic women than the male-centered world of the official court bureaucracy. A crucial caveat, however, is that as the prestige literary form of cursive kana, waka poetry tended to be dominated by men[27] in the formal contexts of banquets, poetry matches, and imperial anthologies, beginning with the *Kokinshū*.

NOTES

1. Unlike all previous eighth-century rulers, Kanmu's father Kōnin (r. 770–781) was descended not from Tenmu (r. 672–686) but from his older brother Tenchi (r. 661–671). Kanmu's mother belonged to a lineage descended from the royal family of the Korean kingdom of Paekche. See Ellen Van Goethem, *Nagaoka: Japan's Forgotten Capital* (Leiden: Brill, 2008).

2. See *Monzen* (*Wen Xuan*): *Bunshōhen, ge*, 199.

3. On the Jian'an era poets see Xiaofei Tian, *The Halberd at Red Cliff: Jian'an and the Three Kingdoms* (Cambridge, MA: Harvard University Asia Center, 2018).

4. On the *Nihongi* lectures see Mathieu Felt, *Rewriting the Past: Textual Structure and Commentarial Legerdemain in Japan's First Official History* (PhD diss., Columbia University, 2017).

5. The earliest extant examples of the term kana (かな) do not appear until the late tenth century, in texts such as *Utsuho monogatari* (970–999) and *The Pillow Book* (*Makura no sōshi*).

6. The oldest instances of these terms date from the late eighteenth and early nineteenth centuries.

7. For a useful overview of the debates over the development of cursive kana writing, see Ogura Shigeji, "Kyū, jū seiki no kana no shotai: Hiragana o chūshin to shite," *Kokuritsu rekishi minzoku hakubutsukan kenkyū hōkoku* (March 2015).

8. The more familiar modern term for standard script, *kaisho* (楷書), came into use from the Song dynasty onward.

9. See Komatsu Hideo, *Nihongo shokishi genron*, rev. ed. (Tokyo: Kasama shoin, 2000).

10. The earliest instance of the term *hiragana* dates from the fifteenth century.

11. See Ouyang Zhongshi and Wen C. Fong, *Chinese Calligraphy*, trans. and ed. Wang Youfen (Princeton, NJ: Yale University Press, 2008), 128–129.

12. See Wen C. Fong, "Chinese Calligraphy: Theory and History," in *The Embodied Image: Chinese Calligraphy from the John B. Elliott Collection* (Princeton, NJ: Princeton University Art Museum, 1999), 29–84.

13. See Ronald Egan, "The Relationship of Calligraphy and Painting to Literature," in *The Oxford Handbook of Classical Chinese Literature (1000 BCE–900 CE)*, ed. Wiebke Denecke, Wai-Yee Li, and Xiaofei Tian, 76–90 (Oxford: Oxford University Press, 2017), 76–90.

14. See Ouyang and Fong, *Chinese Calligraphy*, 215–223.

15. On letter-writing and friendship in China, see Antje Richter, *Letters and Epistolary Culture in Early Medieval China* (Seattle: University of Washington Press, 2013), and also Anna M. Shields, *One Who Knows Me: Friendship and Literary Culture in Mid-Tang China* (Cambridge, MA: Harvard University Asia Center, 2015).

16. The *Wen Xuan* has a category of "Missive and Response Poems" (*zōtōshi*), and the term *zōtō* appears in *Man'yōshū*, vols. 5 and 15.

17. See Komatsu, *Kanabun no kōbun genri* (Tokyo: Kasama shoin, 1997).

18. In the *Man'yōshū*, headnotes and endnotes are written in Literary Sinitic. It is tempting to think that this was simply because cursive kana had not been invented yet. The simple fact that cursive kana was available in the early tenth century, however, does not fully explain why it was used to write the headnotes and endnotes in the *Kokinshū*, particularly given that the prose sections of many commentaries and poetry contest judgments written long after the *Kokinshū* are written in variant forms of Literary Sinitic.

19. Prose writings related to poetry include letters, poetic diaries based on correspondence (such as the *Kagerō Diary* and its precursors), fictionalized tales based on a historical character (such as the *Tales of Ise*),

fantastic tales that incorporate other-worldly elements (such as the *Tale of the Bamboo Cutter*), and of course commentaries.

20. Another way to put this is that Literary Sinitic is a cosmopolitan register that can be read "in Chinese" and in other languages (such as Japanese), whereas kana can be read only in vernacular Japanese. For a more extensive discussion of this, see David B. Lurie, *Realms of Literacy: Early Japan and the History of Writing* (Cambridge, MA: Harvard University Asia Center, 2011), 323–334.

21. See *Tosa nikki* in *Shin Nihon koten bungaku taikei 24*, ed. Hasegawa Masaharu et al (Tokyo: Iwanami shoten, 1989). The word *wotokomoji* appears on page 17, in the context of an anecdote about Abe no Nakamaro. The opening sentence of the *Tosa Diary* on page 3 contains a pun on the words *wotokomoji* and *womunamoji*.

22. See Ogura "Kyū, jū seiki no kana no shotai."

23. See "Hahakigi," *in Genji monogatari, Shinpen Nihon bungaku zenshū 20*, ed. Abe Akio et al. (Tokyo: Shōgakkan, 1994), 89.

24. Note, of course, that Literary Sinitic had informal registers, too.

25. On *wonnade* and *wotokode*, see Harada Yoshioki. "Otokode, onnade meigi kō," in *Heian jidai bungaku goi kenkyū, zokuhen* (Tokyo: Kazama shobō, 1973), 1–11.

26. This passage is discussed in detail in Ogura, "Kyū, jū seiki no kana no shotai."

27. As indeed was the development of calligraphic kana styles—the earliest extant examples of which are fragments of the *Kokinshū* manuscripts.

Chapter Three

THE CONCEPTION AND STRUCTURE OF THE *KOKINSHŪ*

THE *KOKINSHŪ* is presented in its two prefaces as an anthology that was compiled by imperial decree in the year 905. Although the precedent cited for this is the compilation of the *Man'yōshū* during the Nara period,[1] its more recent models included the three collections of Sinitic poetry compiled during the reigns of Saga and Junna in the early ninth century, whose prefaces note that they were compiled by imperial decree. Sinitic poetry was the preeminent literary genre at the Heian court, and the objective of the *Kokinshū* was to elevate waka to a comparable level of prestige.

A crucial development in both the practice of Sinitic poetry and the development of waka at the Heian court was the transmission to Japan in the mid-ninth century of the collected poems of the Tang poet Bai Juyi (772–846). The popularity and influence of Bai's works on subsequent Sinitic poetry composition in Japan is hard to overstate. The foremost Sinitic poets of the mid-ninth-century Heian court—figures such as Ono no Takamura (802–852), Shimada no Tadaomi (828–892), and Miyako no Yoshika (834–879)—were all deeply influenced by Bai, as were Tadaomi and Yoshika's star students who became the leading cultural figures of the court in the late ninth century at the time the *Kokinshū* was being compiled—Sugawara no Michizane (845–903) and Ki no Haseo (845–912). The influence of Bai Juyi's poetry is evident in the waka topics assigned at poetry contests held during Emperor Uda's reign (r. 887–897), the largest of which was "The Empress's Song Contest in the Kanpyō Era," a competition in one hundred rounds (two hundred poems) held sometime between 889 and 894 at the residence of Uda's mother Empress Hanshi (833–900). The contest was organized into five sets of twenty rounds, with the first four sets dedicated to the spring, summer, autumn, winter and the last set to love poetry. The structure of this poetry contest had a powerful influence on the organization of the *Kokinshū*, which also included fifty-four of its poems.

A clear sign that waka poetry was being elevated and compared with Sinitic poetry in the period leading up to the compilation of the *Kokinshū* is the existence of poetry collections that translate one form into the other. For example, *The Newly Selected Collection of Myriad Ages* (*Shinsen Man'yōshū*), whose compilation is traditionally attributed to Sugawara no Michizane, is a short two-volume anthology of more than two hundred waka poems—most of which are from the "Empress's Song Contest in the Kanpyō Era"—with accompanying "translations" into Sinitic seven-graph quatrain poems.[2] Another text known as *Topic Waka* or *The Chisato Collection* (*Kudai waka* or

Chisato shū, 894), compiled by the poet Ōe no Chisato, is a collection of one hundred and twenty lines from Sinitic poems by Bai Juyi and Yuan Zhen, which have been creatively "translated" or paraphrased by Chisato into waka poems. That is, Chisato composed his waka using the couplet lines from Bai's poems as if they were assigned topics. It is in the context of such experiments that the prefaces to the *Kokinshū* anthology, presented to Uda's son Emperor Daigo (r. 897–930), explicitly argue for the elevation of vernacular waka poetry to the level of Sinitic poetry.

Although the *Kokinshū* claims to be a kind of sequel to the *Man'yōshū* (the Mana Preface notes that the title of an early draft of the *Kokinshū* was "The *Man'yōshū* Continued"), it is a very different kind of anthology. Its organization into twenty volumes appears to be modeled on the *Man'yōshū*, but it is less than one fourth of the length. Although the *Man'yōshū* has a significant number of "long poems" (*chōka*), the conception of waka in the *Kokinshū* is essentially synonymous with the five-measure thirty-one-syllable form whose origin its prefaces trace back to the god Susano-o's mythical poem in the *Nihon shoki*.[3] Most obviously, the *Kokinshū* is a collection of poetry written in cursive kana, and in this respect, it is very different from the various logographic and phonographic experiments in writing vernacular poetry in the *Man'yōshū*.

This difference in written form is probably an important reason why the *Kokinshū*'s conception of poetic composition and authorship differs quite strikingly from that of the *Man'yōshū*. The term for "author" in the *Man'yōshū* is *sakusha* (作者), which literally means "maker," and is the usual Sinitic term for "literary author" in the sense of the creator of a discrete piece of work.

This term, which arose together with the emergence of literary writing as a bibliographical category in medieval China, is also used in the three early Heian imperial anthologies of Sinitic poetry. The *Kokinshū*, however, never uses the term *sakusha*, and with one single exception,[4] it does not refer to poetic composition as "making" either. The word for composition in the *Kokinshū* is *yomu*, which literally means "read" or "recite," and the term for "author" is *yomibito* (literally, "reciting person"). Etymologically *yomu* means to "call out" units one by one and thus also "to count." In other words, to "compose" in thirty-one kana graphs means to "call out" or "recite" thirty-one units of sound (syllables). In the *Kokinshū* manuscripts, *yomibito* is written with the graph 読, meaning "to read a written text out loud."[5] This term for composition is therefore one that emphasizes the reciting of song, as opposed to its written creation. *Yomu* is also a reading of the graph 詠, which in its Sinitic usage originally means "recite" or "chant," and is used specifically for the reciting of versified language, and by extension as a verb to mean "poetic composition" (i.e., the composing of prosodic units) and as a noun to refer to a poem. In addition, the graph 詠 is also used to mean "poetic composition on a particular topic," as attested by the existence of a genre of "composing poems on things" (詠物) that was established during the Southern Dynasties and was further popularized during the Tang. In other words, the ideal notion of "authorship" in the *Man'yōshū* points to the creation of a discrete piece of versified Sinographic writing, whereas the *Kokinshū* conception of composition as "reciting" emphasizes the "counting out" of thirty-one graphs of kana script to compose a poem on a specific topic.

More than one hundred and twenty authors are named in the *Kokinshū*. With few exceptions, almost all of them were active at some point from the mid-ninth to the early tenth centuries. This period begins with the establishment of the regency system by Fujiwara no Yoshifusa (804–872) in the reigns of Ninmyō (r. 833–850), Montoku (r. 850–58), and Seiwa (r. 858–876), and ends with the reigns of Uda and his son Daigo. One important aspect that distinguishes the *Kokinshū* from both the *Man'yōshū* and the three early Heian anthologies of Sinitic poetry is that it rarely features emperors and other high-ranking figures as authors. In the first volume of the *Kokinshū*, one poem (*KKS* 4) by the Nijō Empress (Fujiwara no Takaiko, consort to Seiwa) and another anonymous poem (*KKS* 7) with a variant attribution to "the former Great Minister" (Takaiko's uncle Fujiwara no Yoshifusa) appear to acknowledge the authority of the Fujiwara regental system. A felicitous spring poem (*KKS* 21) is attributed to Emperor Kōkō (r. 884–887), grandfather to the reigning emperor Daigo, and father to the retired emperor Uda. But Daigo and Uda themselves—the royal figures who were alive at the time of the compilation of the *Kokinshū*—do not have poems in the anthology. Rather, their presence is implicit in the headnotes to poems, as the unnamed patrons who command poets (usually the compilers) to present their compositions. Imperial authority is also implicit in the mention of reign-names when poems were composed, residences where poetry contests were held, and the titles of poetry contests.

The authors active from the mid-ninth century onward include the six exemplary poets "from the recent past" that are named in both *Kokinshū* prefaces and would later become known as the "Six Sages of Song." The most prolific of these are two royal descendants who occupied politically marginal positions—Ariwara no Narihira (825–880) and Archbishop Henjō (816?–890)—and Ono no Komachi (dates unknown), of whom almost nothing is known. Narihira and Komachi in particular play a salient role in the five volumes of love poetry, in which their poems are often used to set a tone or to establish a theme at the beginning of each book. The most notable contemporary authors are figures who played a central role at poetry contests during Uda's reign, including Henjō's son Sosei (dates unknown), the famous calligrapher Fujiwara no Toshiyuki (d. 901 or 907), and Ise (ca. 872?–ca. 938). Most prolific of all are the compilers themselves, a team of four officials from the lower ranks of the aristocracy: Ki no Tsurayuki (872?–945?), his older cousin Ki no Tomonori (dates unknown), Ōshikōchi no Mitsune (dates unknown), and Mibu no Tadamine (dates unknown). Roughly one-third of the poems with named authors is attributed to one of the four compilers—a total of two hundred and forty-three poems, which is a little less than one-fourth of the entire collection—and the main compiler Tsurayuki is the author of one in seven of the poems that have named authors in the *Kokinshū*.

The general anthologies compiled during the Six Dynasties that were known in Japan—foremost among them the *Wen Xuan* but also *Yutai Xin'yong*—were collections, usually organized by genre, of the most notable literary authors of the past, some of whom had personal collections that were named after them. They also included a small number of unattributed poems under the heading of "old poems" (*gushi*) or "music bureau" (*yuefu*). The cultural value of such anonymous poems was that they were old or popular, dating from a time before the emergence of literary composition and court poetry as an independent genre and the cataloguing of poetry collections named after their authors.

Both the *Man'yōshū* and the *Kokinshū* include a vastly greater number of anonymous poems than their Sinitic counterparts. In the case of the *Kokinshū*, more than one-third of its poems are marked as "composer unknown."[6] In one sense, the function of anonymous poems in the *Kokinshū* is similar to that of Sinitic anthologies, albeit on a much larger scale. The fact that a handful of these poems are followed by endnotes suggesting possible attributions to Nara-period poets, such as Hitomaro, "the Nara emperor," and several other prominent courtiers of the Nara period makes it clear that they are meant to represent the "ancient" poems of the collection.[7] These attributions are for the most part apocryphal—none of the poems attributed to Hitomaro in the *Kokinshū* appear in the *Man'yōshū*. Yet even if some "composer unknown" poems feature diction that is more characteristic of eighth-century waka, a significant number of them use *Man'yōshū*-style phrases, and a handful are either identical to poems in the *Man'yōshū* or are variant versions. Unlike Sinitic anthologies, which place anonymous poems at the beginning of volumes or genre-sections to organize their poems historically, the *Kokinshū* volumes intersperse the "composer unknown" poems with the compositions of named poets. Thus, instead of a linear narrative of poetic development from ancient times to the present, readers of the anthology are presented with a constant alternating of new poems by named authors with old poems that are anonymous.

The *Kokinshū* is an anthology with a clear structure and orga-
nization.[8] The bulk of the collection is made up of its two largest
categories of poems, seasonal songs (volumes 1–6, 342 poems)
and love songs (volumes 11–15, 393 poems). The organization of
poems according to the progress of seasons in the first six vol-
umes is echoed in the five love volumes, which are organized
according to the stages of a love affair, from its initial blossoming
to its eventual fading. The remaining volumes tend to be shorter
and feature categories of poems composed on specific types of
occasion, such as "Felicitous Songs" (volume 7, 21 poems), "Fare-
well Songs" (volume 8, 40 poems), "Travel Songs" (volume 9,
15 poems),[9] or "Lament Songs" (volume 16, 33 poems). "Names
of Things" (volume 10, 46 poems) is dedicated to compositions
on the topic of specific assigned words that must be included
in the poems as hidden puns. Two volumes of "Miscellaneous
Songs" (volumes 17–18, 137 poems) include poems on topics or
occasions that do not fit into any of the other categories, includ-
ing songs composed at informal banquets and festivals, and
featuring topics such as exile, aging, or renouncing the secular
world. "Miscellaneous Forms" (volume 19, 67 poems) includes
five "long poems" (one anonymous, three by the compilers, and
one by Ise on the death of her mistress, the Shichijō Empress),
four *sedōka*, with the remainder dedicated to "eccentric songs"
(*haikaika*)—that is, poems that are judged to breach the rules
of decorous diction or subject matter. The last volume (volume
20, 32 poems) is divided into sections on "Royal Songs from
the Great Bureau of Songs" "Divine Ritual Songs and "Songs
of the East," which include songs congratulating the emperor
on his accession. Some have argued that the overall structure of

the *Kokinshū* was modeled on the Heian imperial government's division into human and ritual administrations (the Council of State and the Council of Gods): the anthology's first nineteen volumes collect the poetry of human affairs and the last volume is dedicated to songs related to ritual acts of the emperor. In this regard, it is perhaps significant that, with one single exception, the songs collected in volume 20 are neither attributed to an author or marked as "composer unknown," suggesting that they were regarded as belonging to the ritual realm.[10]

The fundamental themes and order of the *Kokinshū* are determined by the first six seasonal volumes. This structure has a precedent in the *Man'yōshū*, in which volumes 8 and 10 are each organized into four sections according to season. It is also likely that the organization of the *Kokinshū* was shaped by more recent practices, including the seasonal festivals held at the residence of the Fujiwara regents, and poetry contests sponsored by Emperor Uda. Headnotes to poems in the *Kokinshū*, as well as evidence from other contemporary sources, suggest that the poetry contests (*uta awase*) that took place during Uda's reign had created new kinds of cultural spaces that borrowed the sovereign-centered ritual structure of the court but transformed it into something quite different. The *Kokinshū*'s seasonal order depends on the framework of the imperial calendar, but it operates in a different environment than the official ritual spaces of the imperial palace, in which court rank and official posts determined social position. The private formal spaces of the mansions, gardens, and mountain retreats of regents, retired emperors, and other royal figures were socially organized with greater emphasis on relations of kinship and patronage. Gustav

Heldt has argued that whereas official court festivals (*sechie*) and banquets (*kyōen*) were attended by the male courtiers who served their imperial sovereign, poetry contests represented a new form of household-centered community that included women as well as men.[11]

It is unclear to what extent the *Kokinshū* text is a faithful representation of this new form of community, given that the four low-ranking male compilers occupy such a prominent place in the collection and that remarkably few poems are written by women, particularly when compared to later imperial anthologies. Although women represent a little less than one-quarter of the named poets in the *Kokinshū*, the number of poems by women accounts for only 6 percent of the compositions by named poets.[12] Komachi, the only woman among the six poets mentioned in the Kana Preface, has eighteen poems in the *Kokinshū* (second only to Narihira's thirty, more than Henjō's seventeen), and Ise, the most prolific woman poet of Uda and Daigo's reigns, has twenty-two poems included. Given, however, the few lower-ranking women among named poets in the *Kokinshū* (i.e., women of the same rank as the compilers), it is also possible that a significant number of anonymous poems in the *Kokinshū* were composed by women but were left unattributed. In other words, the low figure of 6 percent may be more of an indication of whether women were being credited as authors in poetry contests and in anthologies than of whether they composed much poetry. If the former were so, it would mean that the *Kokinshū* represented an opportunity for male officials of the lower ranks, such as the compilers, to make a name for themselves, but not for women of the same rank.

As its title suggests, the main theme of the *Kokinwakashū* is the cultural memory of the court, the sustaining thread of which is the imperial lineage, whose maintenance is in turn entrusted to the Fujiwara regents. The cyclical seasonal structure of the anthology is given depth by its "ancient and modern" conception, which has precedents in the *Man'yōshū*, as well as in medieval Sinitic conceptualizations of poetic history.[13] By constantly alternating ancient poems with their own compositions and those of their contemporaries, the *Kokinshū* compilers create a constant dialogue between the present and the past and a continuous theme of "revering the old and desiring the new," to quote the final words of the Kana Preface.

NOTES

1. The *Man'yōshū* has no preface, so the circumstances of its compilation are unknown, but despite what the *Kokinshū* compilers may have believed, all evidence suggests that it was *not* imperially commissioned. The present consensus is that the poet Ōtomo no Yakamochi was the main final compiler of a collection that had been put together gradually by multiple people since the beginning of the eighth century.

2. Numerous sources in both Japanese and English state that the waka in *Shinsen Man'yōshū* are written "in *man'yōgana*" or even "in kana," but this is incorrect. The compiler of *Shinsen Man'yōshū* took the poems from the poetry contests—which are presumed to have been cursive kana texts—and rewrote them into *Man'yōshū*-style logographic texts, that is, as full-form Sinographs in a primarily logographic style supplemented by phonographs to write particles. There are, however, two major differences between the written style of *Shinsen Man'yōshū* and the logographic volumes of the *Man'yōshū*: (1) the supplementary phonographs make no distinction of the so-called *kō* and *otsu* vowel-type distinctions that are characteristic of Asuka- and Nara-period Japanese but had disappeared by the Heian period; and (2) the supplementary phonographs make no

distinction, as phonographs in Nara period texts do, between voiced and unvoiced sounds. This second difference strongly suggests that the *Shinsen Man'yōshū* was a logographic transcription of what were originally phonographic kana texts.

3. The only exceptions are relegated to the "Miscellaneous Forms" section of vol. 19: five *chōka* as instances of a rarely practiced virtuoso form (three are by the compilers) and four *sedōka* (three are anonymous and one is by Tsurayuki) as pseudo-antique compositions.

4. The Mana Preface uses the graph 作 (to make) on one occasion to refer to waka composition—when it notes at the beginning that in the age of the gods "there was still no waka composition" (和歌未作). It then continues: "The first time there was a composition (詠) in thirty-one letters was when the god Susano-o arrived in the Land of Izumo." From then onward, the preface uses the graph 詠 to refer to poetic composition. The Kana Preface always uses the term *yomu* to refer to poetry composition.

5. This graph is used late in the *Man'yōshū*, but only in the sense of "reading" a poem composed by someone else.

6. A similar ratio applies to the *Man'yōshū*, which dedicates seven of its twenty volumes exclusively to unattributed poems (vols. 7, 10–14, and 16), whereas its remaining fourteen volumes (vols. 1–6, 8–9, 15, and 17–20) also include some poems whose author is given as "unknown" or "unidentified."

7. This "Nara emperor" cannot be identified as any particular Nara-period ruler but appears to represent a figure of imperial authority contemporary to Hitomaro.

8. Compared with the *Man'yōshū*, which was put together gradually by different people over a period of almost a century, the compilation of the *Kokinshū* was relatively short and straightforward. That being said, the process must have taken at least eight years, as indicated by the fact that the *Kokinshū*'s two prefaces are dated to the year 905, but the anthology includes poems from Retired Emperor Uda's Teiji Palace Poetry Contest in 913. Although the prefaces are addressed to Emperor Daigo, it is likely that the interests of Retired Emperor Uda and Daigo's Minister of the Left Fujiwara no Tokihira also helped shape the anthology.

9. Unlike the *Man'yōshū*, which includes many poems on travel to represent the extent of imperial cultural influence beyond the capital to the provinces, the poems of the *Kokinshū* are for the most part set within the

confines of the capital. One clear sign of this is the fact that there are far more poems in "Farewell Songs," volume 8, which are for the most part set in and around the capital, than in "Travel Songs," volume 9.

10. The exception is the last poem in the *Kokinshū*, which is attributed to Fujiwara no Toshiyuki.

11. See Gustav Heldt, *The Pursuit of Harmony: Poetry and Power in Early Heian Japan* (Ithaca, NY: Cornell University Press, 2008).

12. See Gian Piero Persiani, *Waka After the Kokinshū: Anatomy of a Cultural Phenomenon* (PhD diss., Columbia University, 2013), 40.

13. An example of this is the *Ancient and Modern Poetry Garden Prime Blossoms*, a no-longer-extant nineteen-volume collection attributed to Xiao Tong, compiler of the *Wen Xuan*.

Chapter Four

TOPICS OF COMPOSITION

JUST AS ALL POEMS in the *Kokinshū*, with the exception of poems in volume 20, include the name of an author (or the phrase "composer unknown"), they are also preceded by headnotes that either convey some information about the composition or are marked as "topic unknown" (*dai shirazu*). The term *dai* (題) is most often understood in relation to the term *daiei* (題詠), which means "composition on (assigned) topics" in a manner that would be faithful to the conventional treatment of the given topic in the past.[1] This specific understanding of the term dates from the late eleventh and twelfth centuries onward, when the tradition of waka poetry written in cursive kana had been well established. At the time this tradition was first initiated and the *Kokinshū* was compiled, however, the term *dai* as it appears in the phrase *dai shirazu* in *Kokinshū* headnotes was a capacious concept that could include a variety of different kinds of paratextual information.

Its primary sense, which derived from Sinitic poetic discourse, was that of any topic for poetry composition assigned at a formal event, such as a banquet or poetry contest. The practice of composing poetry on specific topics can be traced to the Sinitic tradition of "composing on objects" (*yong wu* 詠物, or *eibutsu* in Japanese), which developed during the Six Dynasties and the early Tang. These were compositions in which poets showcased their ingenuity, often at court banquets, by describing the effects and associations of various natural and artificial objects.[2] One collection of such "compositions on objects" that was particularly influential in Japan from Saga's reign onward was the early Tang poet Li Jiao's (ca. 646–715) *Hundred and Twenty Compositions*, a sequence of poems on single graph topics arranged in a systematic order much like that of a classified encyclopedia.[3] Designed as a primer for composition, the *Hundred and Twenty Compositions* includes twelve categories of objects with ten topics each. Half of the topics are heavenly and earthly objects (i.e., what we would refer to as "natural"), and the other half consists of valuable human-made objects (what we might call "artificial"). The natural objects are arranged as a cosmological sequence, ranging from "heavenly" objects (sun, moon, stars, wind, clouds . . .) to earthly landscape objects (mountains, rocks, fields . . .) to plants, trees, birds, and beasts. The artificial objects are organized as a ranked list of courtly material possessions ranging from various types of buildings and transportation vehicles, to furniture, to objects related to literary writing, to weapons and other martial accessories, to musical instruments, and to precious metals and textiles. As their encyclopedic arrangement suggests, these topical pretexts for literary composition were first and foremost lexical items: they represented the names of things, along with all their textual and literary associations. It is no coincidence that *yongwu* poetry developed at the same time as classified encyclopedias (*leishu*), which summarized the literate knowledge deemed essential for court officials by collecting essential quotations on topics and arranging them into a hierarchical order of categories centered on a heavenly sanctioned sovereign and the spatiotemporal organization of the imperial realm. In a similar manner, *yongwu* poetry focused on the various natural and artificial objects, each imbued with conventional metaphorical or allegorical associations, which together made up the natural and social world of the imperial court. In formal settings, such as court banquets, the textual existence of this literary world of poetic objects made it possible, whether through the presence of the physical objects, by means of simulated garden landscapes or through visual media, such as dioramas or screen paintings, to summon their poetic associations or allegorical senses into the social space of the gathering.

Discrete instances of such topical composition appear frequently in the extant Japanese collections of Sinitic poetry from the Nara and Early Heian periods. Since at least the mid-eighth century, topics and topical organization were also a feature of waka poetry. Perhaps inspired by Li Jiao's *One Hundred Compositions*, or by other no-longer-extant Sinitic *yongwu* collections, the *Man'yōshū* includes encyclopedic sequences of waka "composed on objects" (詠物) in its seventh and tenth volumes. Volume 7 includes topical sequences that map out the natural world (heaven, moon, clouds, mountains, hills, rivers, dew, leaves, moss, grass, birds), and volume 10 is organized into seasonal sections that are in turn subdivided into topics. Topics for composition were thus organized into a spatiotemporal order centered on the imperial capital and calendar.

The dual function of poetic topics as elements that make up the courtly poetic world and also serve as vessels for specific conventional metaphorical or allegorical senses was codified in the *Man'yōshū*. The sequences of "Composing on Objects" in volume 7 are contrasted in a section of "Metaphorical Poems" that appear later in the volume with poems on "Conveying Through Objects" (寄物), an innovative category that appears to be original to the *Man'yōshū* and that reappears in volume 10. The implicit metaphorical associations in the "Composing on Objects" (詠物) poems in the "Miscellaneous Songs" (*zōka* 雑歌) sections of each season are counterbalanced in the "Exchanges" (*sōmon* 相聞) sections of each season through the explicit metaphorical intent in the title "Conveying Through Objects." This category appears once again as a subgenre of the *sōmon* love poetry exchanges in volumes 11 and 12 in sections that have the even more explicit title of "Expressing Feelings by Conveying Them Through Objects" (*kibutsu chinshi* 寄物陳思), which is the counterpart of the more straightforward category of "Stating Emotions Directly" (*seijutsu shinsho* 正述心緒) that precedes it in the same volume.

By the late ninth century, it appears to have been well established that the primary topics of thirty-one syllable waka poetry were the seasons and love. The earliest waka poetry contests for which written records survive date from the reign of Emperor Uda (r. 887–997), one or two decades before the compilation of the *Kokinshū*. The so-called Minister of Popular Affairs Yukihira Song Contest (*Minbukyō Yukihira ke uta awase*, ca. 885–887?) had twelve rounds, of which the first ten were on the specific topic of "the cuckoo bird" and the last two were on the topical category of "love" (in one manuscript, the topic is described more specifically as "love unmet"). The "Rear Palace Chrysanthemum Contest" (ca. 889–891?) was, as its name indicates, dedicated in its entirety to this single topic. The "Prince Koresada Mansion Song Contest" (ca. 889–894?) was dedicated exclusively to poems on the theme of autumn, even if it did not explicitly announce autumn as the topic. The largest of these contests, the "Empress's Song Contest in the Kanpyō Era" (ca. 889–894?), was organized into five topics: spring, summer, autumn, winter, and love. All of these were either topical categories or subtopics that represented the larger topical category—the cuckoo bird stands for summer, and chrysanthemums represent autumn. In all of these contests, the primary emphasis was on seasonal topics, with the category of love occupying a secondary position in those cases in which it appears.

These poetry contests that took place throughout the two decades before the compilation of the *Kokinshū* exerted a profound influence on its organizational structure—in particular, on the seasonal order of its first six volumes, each of which includes subtopics of seasonal "earthly" objects that are "seen" (such as cherry blossoms or autumn leaves) or "heard" (birds and other animals). These seasonal topics and subtopics reappear frequently in the other two major topical categories of "love" (volumes 11–15) and "miscellaneous" (17–18), as well as in the individual volumes dedicated to poetry marking different kinds of social occasions (volumes 7–9 and 16), and volumes dedicated to specialized kinds of compositions (volumes 10, 19, and 20). Somewhat less obviously, natural topics that are *not seasonal*, such as rivers, mountains, the moon, or rain, are present throughout all of the volumes in the *Kokinshū* and therefore perform a key function of integrating all the volumes into a whole.

The dual categorization of all poems as having a topic and an author is a unifying frame that is shared across the various volumes of the *Kokinshū*. That being said, the fact that topical classification is present throughout the anthology does not mean it is in any way consistent. In fact, poem headnotes in the *Kokinshū* vary greatly in both content and length. One type of headnote simply describes the topic of composition, at times succinctly, such as "Composed on falling snow" (*KKS* 9, Tsurayuki) or "Composed on geese returning" (*KKS* 31, Ise), or in a slightly more elaborate manner, "Composed on snow falling and covering the trees" (*KKS* 6, Sosei). Some include the compositional setting, "Composed on the willow tree in the Great Temple of the West" (*KKS* 27, Henjō), but they provide no indication of the specific occasion on which the poems were composed. Other headnotes provide both the topic of composition and some indication of the occasion, as is the case with "At the Eastern Prince's Palace, composed upon seeing cherry blossoms fall and run down the stream" (*KKS* 81, Sugano no Takayo), in which the setting in the crown prince's palace suggests a formal social context. A different kind of example is found in "Composed when he heard the cry of the geese and was reminded of someone who had left for Koshi"

(*KKS* 30, Mitsune), in which the occasion of composition is depicted from a more intimate perspective. As these instances suggest, the concept of "topic" operating in the *Kokinshū* was one that encompassed both the lexical "object" or main theme of a poem, as well as what was known or what the compilers decided to note about the occasional circumstances of its composition.

Many *Kokinshū* headnotes, moreover, do not describe the topic at all and indicate *only* the occasion. This is the case with poems that were originally composed at poetry contests, as indicated by the headnote to "Songs from the Empress's Song Contest in the Kanpyō Era" (*KKS* 12–15). The topic of the poems in the original contest was simply "Spring," which is indicated in the *Kokinshū* implicitly by their inclusion in the first spring volume. Similarly, the songs from the "Prince Koresada Mansion Song Contest" are all included in the autumn volumes (the topic of the entire original poetry contest), poems from the "Maiden Flower Contest" are included in the sequence of maiden flower poems at the end of the first autumn volume, and poems from "the Kanpyō Era Chrysanthemum Contest" are included in the sequence of chrysanthemum poems in the second autumn volume. In these cases, the strategy of the compilers seems to have been to record the name of the poetry contest at which the poem was submitted in place of the "topic" and then to allow the topic to be made evident by the poem's placement in a particular volume or section of a volume in the *Kokinshū*.

Scholars often refer to poetry composed at formal social occasions like banquets or poetry contests as *hare*, a term first used in the early thirteenth century to mean "formal," "decorous," "appropriate," "seemly," "refined," "elegant," "special," or "felicitous" (the original sense of the graph refers to a clear sky with good weather). *Hare* is sometimes contrasted with the term *ke*, meaning "ordinary, everyday, vulgar." These terms are not used anywhere in the *Kokinshū* anthology, but they do appear from the early thirteenth century onward in commentaries and poetry contest judgments. From their use, modern scholars have extrapolated a contrast between the "formal" or "public" poetry that was composed for poetry contests, banquets, and other social occasions, and the "private" or "informal" poetry of amorous or intimate contexts. Scholars have extended this *hare/ke* distinction to describe the anthological organization of the *Kokinshū* and subsequent imperial waka anthologies in terms of a contrast between the "felicitous" seasonal volumes and the everyday social (amorous) use of poetry exhibited in the love volumes.

Note, however, that this distinction between *hare* and *ke* poems, and its associated binary contrasts of formal public occasions versus informal private circumstances, is for the most part a modern conceptualization. In the medieval texts in which the terms first appear, *hare* indeed is used to describe poetic compositions that are appropriate to formal occasions, but there is no such thing as a "*ke* poem" (*ke no uta*). The term *ke* simply refers to diction that is inappropriate for *hare* poems composed for a formal social context. In other words, waka scholars and commentators from the thirteenth century onward believed that poetry composed on formal social occasions should employ decorous and elevated diction, but they gave no indication in any of their writings of the existence of the idea of two distinct and contrasting modes of poetry—one public and formal, the other private and informal.[4]

A more apt distinction is that between social occasions that were presided over by an imperial authority in which formal poetry is "humbly presented" (*tatematsurikeru*) and that of informal written correspondence, which is often explicitly marked in the *Kokinshū* as poems that are "sent" to (*okurikeru*, or more commonly *tsukawashikeru*) or "received" from (*okosetarikeru*) lovers and friends, as well as implicitly denoted in the many headnotes that depict the context of composition as an amorous exchange (in the love volumes) or as friendly communication (in the miscellaneous volumes). What defines a formal occasion for poetry composition in the *Kokinshū* is the presence, explicit or implicit, of a presiding authority—often the emperor, sometimes a retired emperor or an empress-consort, or at times an imperial prince—acting as patron of the event. This is the case with an imperial banquet, or with an occasion like a poetry contest, in which poems are composed by subjects in response to topics assigned in the presence of the sovereign. Such poems tend to be included in the seasonal volumes as well as in the volumes that feature poems on social occasions, such as "Felicitous Poems" or "Laments." It is significant that a handful of *Kokinshū* headnotes describe the assignment of a topic by the sovereign without mentioning the topic itself or the occasion. This is the case with several of Tsurayuki's poems (*KKS* 22, 25–26, and 342), all of which are introduced by the same identical phrase, "Composed and presented when he was commanded to present a song," in which the honorific verb form of "commanded" and the humilific verb form of "presented" (*tatematsurikeru*) clearly indicate the presence of the sovereign.

Other *Kokinshū* headnotes illustrate the degrees of formality that surround all acts of poetic composition when the sovereign or an imperial figure are present. This is the case in the four instances in the anthology in which the actual term "topic" (*dai*) is used in a headnote and described in detail. Two of these date from Emperor Montoku's reign and describe topics for poems to accompany paintings: one introducing two poems composed in the quarters of the Crown Prince's Consort (Fujiwara no Takaiko, who would later become the Nijō Empress), "on the topic of autumn leaves flowing down the Tatsuta River as painted on a picture on a folding screen" (*KKS* 293–294, Sosei and Narihira), and the other on the occasion of Montoku paying a visit to his ladies-in-waiting to see a painted scene of "a waterfall cascading" (*KKS* 930). The other two are topics assigned by the Retired Emperor Uda on the occasion of an excursion to the West River (also known as the Ōi River), and the poems are both by *Kokinshū* compilers: Tsurayuki dutifully composes a poem on the assigned topic of "cranes standing on the bars in the river" (*KKS* 919), and Mitsune complies with Uda's outlandish request for a poem on "monkeys howling in a mountain ravine" (*KKS* 1067). Although these occasions for composition take place in informal social spaces, they possess a certain degree of formality by virtue of the fact that the poems are composed by subjects in response to the presence of an imperial figure.

The topics of these four poems do not simply feature an object (autumn leaves, waterfall, cranes, monkeys), but an object in action within a visual (and aural) setting—autumn leaves *flowing down the Tatsuta River*, a *cascading* waterfall, cranes *standing on the bars in the river*, and monkeys *howling in a mountain ravine*. In other words, the "topics" assigned for composition consist of objects situated within a scene that has movement or action. Such topical scenic situations are similar to those of *kudai waka*, in which waka poems were composed not simply on an item of the poetic lexicon, but on a more elaborate topic provided by an excerpted verse line (*ku*) or couplet of Sinitic poetry exemplifying the canonical treatment of a specific topic. For instance, in Ōe no Chisato's *Kudai waka*, which was organized into eight categories, including the four seasons, "Wind and Moon," "Excursions," "Miscellaneous," and "Expressing Feelings," most of the topic lines were selected from poems by Bai Juyi or Yuan Zhen and describe scenes such as "attracted by the warbler's cry, I've come here beneath the blossoms" (from Bai Juyi's poem "Spring River") or "the wind overturns the white waves into a thousand blossom petals" (from Bai Juyi's "Gazing into the Distance from a River Tower"). These topics or combinations of topics (the warbler and the blossoms, white waves and blossoms) are contextualized into landscape scenes, some that merely imply an observer, and others in which the first-person human protagonists are part of the scene.

An example of a poem composed on the topic of a scene that includes a fictional first-person protagonist is attributed to the compiler Ōshikōchi no Mitsune:

Presented when asked to compose on the topic of a picture on a folded screen in the Pavilion Palace in which a man who is about to cross a river has stopped his horse beneath a tree from which scarlet leaves are falling

Mitsune

I will stop here
    and cross after I watch
the scarlet leaves:
    though they fall like the rain
    the waters will not rise (*KKS* 305)

The setting of the "Pavilion Palace" indicates that the authority who presides over the occasion and is the recipient of Mitsune's presentation of the poem is Retired Emperor Uda. Mitsune is assigned the task of composing a poem in the voice of the horse-rider to animate the scene in the painting. In this composite scene created by the painting and the poem, the man is about to cross the river when he is moved to compose a poem by the sight of the scarlet leaves in the water. There is no imperial presence here *within* the scene created by the poem-painting; instead, it depicts a solitary, contemplative moment, not unlike those suggested in other headnotes in the *Kokinshū* seasonal volumes in which the poem is not composed in response to an assignment at a social occasion, but rather is inspired by something the poet sees or hears in a solitary or intimate context. Another example, also by Mitsune, was cited earlier: "Composed when he heard the cry of the geese and was reminded of someone who had left for Koshi" (*KKS* 30). Headnotes such as these, which portray the poets as being moved to compose by "the things they see and hear," to quote the opening words of Tsurayuki's Kana Preface, can also include peer-to-peer social situations, as in the following headnote by Tsurayuki: "Composed when he saw that the cherry blossoms growing at a certain person's house had begun to bloom" (*KKS* 49).

There is a clear difference between a descriptive record of the circumstances of a poetic composition during a formal social event presided over by the sovereign—one that could have been recorded by any of the people attending, and that of *KKS* 30, which is written in the form of personal anecdote and describes the thoughts of the poet himself. The painting in *KKS* 305 is a topic that is assigned to the poet by the sovereign, whereas the topic of a poem such as *KKS* 30 is either self-assigned, if the author of the headnote also happens to be the author of the poem, or was retrospectively assigned, in cases in which the compilers write headnotes to poems composed by others. In the context of the anthology, however, whether they are written by the poets or by later editors, the function of the "topics" described in the headnotes is to create poetic scenes by contextualizing the poems in the discursive space of the text that Tsurayuki and his coeditors are ostensibly "presenting" to the emperor for his enjoyment.

In some cases, moreover, such as the poem-painting in *KKS* 305, it is not simply that the poem is framed by the headnote but that it relies on it. This is often the case with poems that were written in response to paintings, dioramas, or "live" scenery and that therefore require a description of what the poem was specifically responding to so they may be fully understood outside of the context of the social occasion in which they were composed.[5] But it is also true of headnotes to poems that are written from a more intimate perspective, like the following by Fujiwara no Yoruka:

At a time when she was feeling unwell and had drawn the blinds so as not to be exposed to the wind, she saw a sprig of cherry that had lost its blossoms and composed

Fujiwara Yoruka no Ason

Sitting inside,
> unaware of the passing
of the spring,
> the blossoms I awaited
> have already withered (*KKS* 80)

This headnote does not act merely as additional information but rather as a preface. Without the mini-narrative explaining the poet's illness and mentioning the sprig of cherry, the poem does not quite make sense. In other words, the poem and headnote function together as a narrative unit. *KKS* 80 is not so much a poem with a headnote clarifying the circumstances of composition as it is a short anecdote that includes a poem. Unlike the headnotes of poems composed at social occasions, which are generally written from the perspective of anyone who might have been present, this headnote suggests the perspective of the poet herself. Indeed, we read the headnote as a third-person description primarily due to convention rather than any explicit syntactic marker. It is perfectly possible to read the entire head-note along with the poem in first person: "At a time when I was feeling unwell and had drawn the blinds so as not to be exposed to the wind, I saw a sprig of cherry that had lost its blossoms and composed" (*KKS* 80). Read in this manner, the headnote and poem are indistinguishable from an entry we might see in a poetic kana diary from a later period.

The most notable instances of poems that cannot be made sense of without their accompanying headnotes are those that also appear in *Tales of Ise*, most of which the *Kokinshū* attributes to Narihira.[6] As the following example illustrates, many of these are cases in which the poem is responding to something specific that is mentioned in the headnote:

When Fujiwara no Toshiyuki was seeing a woman who lived in Narihira no Ason's household, he sent a letter with the words, "I promise to come soon, but I am worried it will rain," and upon hearing he had said this, [Narihira] composed in place of the woman

Ariwara no Narihira no Ason

Since I cannot
 ask whether you love me
or love me not,
 the rain which knows my thoughts
 continues to increase (*KKS* 705)

Many more clear examples of this are found among Narihira's poems in the *Kokinshū*, including the famous "Is this not that moon?" (*KKS* 747), the "capital bird" composition (*KKS* 411), or the poem in which he makes fun of a drunk Prince Koretaka (*KKS* 884). Each of these headnotes consist of narrative anecdotes that combine with the poems to constitute what scholars refer to as "poem-tale" (*uta monogatari*) episodes. This is not only the case with poems that also appear in *Tales of Ise*. Many other extended anecdotes, particularly in the love and miscellaneous volumes, do not appear anywhere outside the *Kokinshū* (at least not in any extant text). Like Narihira, the protagonists of these poetic episodes are often famous people of the recent past. For instance, Archbishop Henjō's poems often are accompanied by narrative anecdotes that adopt Henjō's perspective.[7] Other mid- to high-ranking figures, such as Fujiwara no Yoruka (see *KKS* 80), are also the subject of short narrative poetic episodes, some of which take the form of poetic exchanges, as is the case with Yoruka's exchange with Minamoto no Yoshiari (845–897) at the end of the love volume sequence (*KKS* 736–737). On occasion, the compilers add brief narrative frames to their poems and poetic exchanges, both in their love affairs (e.g., *KKS* 478 by Tadamine or *KKS* 479 by Tsurayuki) and in their exchanges with friends (e.g., Tsurayuki's response to his fellow compiler Mitsune in *KKS* 880, or Mitsune's reply to Muneoka no Ōyori in *KKS* 978).

A remarkable exception to this is Ono no Komachi. All but two of her eighteen poems in the *Kokinshū* are marked as "Topic unknown." If Narihira represents the paradigmatic amorous man of the past, Komachi, the vast majority of whose poems are included in the love volumes, stands for the exemplary amorous woman. Although a frequent topic of legends in the medieval period, there appear to have been no narratives about Komachi in the Heian period, or at least none that are extant or that were available to the *Kokinshū* compilers. The only two Komachi poems with headnotes, those to an exchange (*KKS* 556–557) with Abe no Kiyoyuki (825–900) and to a poem (*KKS* 938) sent to Funya no Yasuhide, are written from the perspective of her interlocutors rather than from Komachi's perspective. For the most part, Komachi's poems appear in the *Kokinshū* contextualized by her name, but without any additional topical or circumstantial context.

Note, however, that the "Topic unknown" headnotes function in a context in which the topics of other poems are described in detail. In the seasonal volumes, the interspersing of poems marked as "Topic unknown" with poems that include headnotes describing the circumstances of their composition allows readers to assume a similar range of circumstances for the topic unknown poems. In the case of the love volumes, in which the "Topic unknown" headnote appears most frequently, elaborate headnotes such as those from Narihira's poems provide exemplary instances of the kinds of narrative episodes that other "Topic unknown" poems, such as those attributed to Komachi, might suggest to an imaginative or curious reader. This imaginative reading is encouraged by the fact that some of the compilers' own compositions, particularly in the love volumes, are also marked as "Topic unknown," thus clearly indicating that the phrase can suggest a sense of "no comment" or "would rather not say."[8] More generally, the presence of so many poems in the *Kokinshū* marked both "author unknown" and "topic unknown" is not only a gesture to a past time from which names and circumstances have been lost, but also a sign of anonymous poetic activity in the present (of the *Kokinshū* compilation), as well as an invitation to future readers to read themselves into the poetry of the past.

NOTES

1. For a discussion of the concept of *dai* in English, see Joseph T. Sorensen, *Optical Allusions: Screens, Paintings, and Poetry in Classical Japan (ca. 800–1200)* (Leiden: Brill, 2012).

2. See Stephen Owen, "The Courtly Yongwu," in *The Poetry of the Early Tang* (New Haven, CT: Yale University Press, 1977), 245–55. The preface to the *Wen Xuan* describes *yongwu* rhapsodies as those compositions that "narrate a single event, are composed on a single object, are inspired by wind, clouds, plants, and trees, or look for fish, insects, birds, and beasts."

3. See Brian Steininger, "Li-Jiao's Songs: Commentary Based Reading and the Reception of Tang Poetry in Heian Japan," *East Asian Publishing and Society* 6, no. 2 (2016): 103–129.

4. See Nishiki Hitoshi, "Inseiki uta awase no kōzō to hōhō: 'Ke' kara 'hare' e no waka shikan no hihan," *Nihon bungaku* 43, no. 2 (1994): 24–33. In English, see Gian Piero Persiani, "The Public, the Private, and the In-Between: Poetry Exchanges as Court Diplomacy in Mid-Heian Japan," *Japan Review* 35 (2020): 7–29.

5. For a study of screen poetry in the *Kokinshū* and later anthologies, see Sorensen, *Optical Allusions*.

6. The relationship between the extant *Tales of Ise* text and the *Kokinshū* headnotes is unclear. On the one hand, there is no question that the *Kokinshū* used some early form of the *Tales of Ise* as source material. On the other hand, the extant text of *Tales of Ise* also shows clear signs of having drawn upon the *Kokinshū* headnotes. It is therefore likely that both texts drew upon each other on multiple occasions to arrive at their extant forms.

7. Few of Henjō's poems have "Topic unknown" headnotes (only four of seventeen), and many of them contain elaborate explanations of the circumstances of composition.

8. A similar sense of discretion applies to instances of "Author unknown" in which the headnote makes clear who the author was, such as the Ise Priestess who exchanges poems with Narihira in *Kokinshū* 645–646.

Chapter Five

PROSODY AND RHETORICAL CONVENTIONS

THE *KOKINSHŪ* is an anthology written in a new script, and the form of this script had a profound effect on the rhetorical characteristics of its poetry. A common characteristic of all waka poetry is that its prosody is purely syllabic. That is to say, its prosodic form of five measures in a 5/7/5/7/7 pattern is defined only in terms of the number of syllables per measure. There are no prescribed patterns of syllable duration, stress, or tone. Moreover, unlike Sinitic poetry, or poetry in most European languages, waka lacks end-rhyme. This does not mean that waka poems do not make frequent use of inner rhyme and alliteration, but rather these expressive aspects are specific to individual compositions and are not prosodic conventions or rules.[1] Waka measures are rarely end-stopped, and enjambment—defined as the continuation of a sentence or phrase beyond the end of a line of verse—is the norm, rather than an expressive feature that breaks the rule.[2] An important consequence of this is that the "measures" of waka do not correspond to the "lines of verse" of poetry in European languages, or for that matter to the "measures" of classical Chinese poetry.

The rhythmic unit of waka is in fact the combination of measures of five and seven syllables. Waka are generally analyzed as consisting of two halves: the first three measures of 5/7/5 are referred to as the "beginning" (*moto*) or "upper measures" (*kami no ku*), and the last two (7/7) as the "end" (*sue*) or "lower measures" (*shimo no ku*). Many poems in the *Kokinshū* are indeed structured syntactically with a pause after the third measure, such as the following poem by Ki no Tsurayuki:

袖ひちてむすひし水のこほれるを春たつけふの風やとくらむ

That water where / I drank and drenched my sleeves / before it froze, /

today that spring has come / will it melt in the wind? (*KKS* 2)

Just as common, particularly in older compositions, are poems with a pause after the second measure. A good example of this is found in an anonymous poem that appears in volume 7 of *Man'yōshū* (hereafter *MYS* 1701), which is attributed to Emperor Tenmu's son Prince Yuge (d. 699):

さ夜なかとよはふけぬらしかりかねのきこゆるそらに月わたるみゆ

It seems the night / is moving toward midnight/

as cries of geese/ can be heard in the sky / where the moon has appeared (*KKS* 192)

Another example is attributed to the Nijō Empress:

雪の内に春はきにけり鶯のこほれるなみたいまやとく覧

Spring has arrived / before the snow has gone; /

perhaps now / the warbler's frozen tears / will melt away

at last? (*KKS* 4)

Exceptions to these typical examples include poems that have a break after the first measure; some that have no break at all; or, most unusually, poems in which all five measures are end-stopped, such as the following:

君やこし我やゆきけむおもほえすゆめかうつつかねてか
さめてか

Did you come here? / Or did I go to you? / I do not know. /

Was it real or a dream? / Was I asleep or awake? (*KKS* 645)

Note, however, that in the context of conventional waka rhythm, the effect of end-stopping every measure in this way creates a sense of rhythmic violence—one that fittingly conveys the confusion and bewilderment of the speaker. This effect is further intensified in the final two measures, each of which can be read as being further broken into two questions.

Waka has a number of distinctive conventional poetic techniques. The *Kokinshū* features a few scattered examples of what have come to be known as "pillow-phrases" (*makura kotoba*). These conventional five-syllable (or occasionally four-syllable) epithets of often obscure etymological origin are linked to specific words through semantic association or by means of a pun.

They are characteristic of the *Man'yōshū* but are far less common in the *Kokinshū*. Typical examples include *azusayumi* ("catalpa bow"), which modifies *haru* ("spring" but also "to stretch"); *utsusemi no* ("impermanent"), which modifies *inochi* ("life"); or *hisakata no* ("celestial"), which can modify *hi* ("sun") or *hikari* ("light"). Because pillow-phrases are often ancient, they tend to play an archaicizing role, but they also perform an important prosodic function by combining one five-syllable measure and one seven-syllable measure into a rhythmic phrasal unit consisting of modifier and modified.

A related poetic device is the "preface phrase" (*jo-kotoba*), which also features far more prominently in the *Man'yōshū* than in the *Kokinshū*. Preface phrases usually consist of a description of natural scenery in the first half of a poem that is linked by means of a pun or metaphoric association with the main topic or statement of the poem in the second half. Unlike pillow-phrases, preface phrases are not formulaic epithets and are unique to a particular poem. They also tend to exemplify the Kana Preface's description of waka as relating feelings to things that are seen and heard, as in the following example, which is a variant version of MYS 1655:

> おく山のすかのねしのきふるゆきのけぬといはむこひのし
> けきに

> Just like the snow / that covers the sedge roots / deep in the hills /

> will eventually melt, / I too from love will perish (*KKS* 551)

This rather-straightforward style is also practiced by the *Kokinshū* compilers, as illustrated by Tsurayuki, whose description of the rapids of the Yoshino River leads into a statement of the speaker's feelings of being overwhelmed by longing:

よしの河いはなみたかく行水のはやくそ人をおもひそめてし

    Over the rocks / of the Yoshino River / the water flows /
as rapidly as I /
    began to fall in love (*KKS* 471)

Preface phrases take advantage of the syntactical structure of the Japanese language. The modifying clauses always precede the modified phrase, to create a pivot (which usually falls on the third measure) between the first half of the poem, which often consists of a natural description, and the second half, which usually express the speaker's feelings or attitude. The use of such pivoting third measures is frequent in a great many poems in the *Kokinshū*, such as the following example by Tsurayuki, in which the phrase "faintly I saw" (ほのかにもみてし) refers both to what precedes it (the mountain cherries) and what follows it (the person whom the speaker loves):

山さくら霞のまよりほのかにも見てし人こそこひしかりけれ

    Mountain cherries / through the gaps in the haze / faintly
I saw /
    only the briefest glimpse / of the one whom I love (*KKS* 479)

This kind of multilayering is formalized in what is by far the most common and characteristic poetic device in the *Kokin-shū*, the pun or *kakekotoba*, the historical development of which is closely related to the preface phrase. Waka in the *Kokinshū* engage in puns to a greater degree and in a more playful and unexpected manner than in any other anthology. The style of script in which the *Kokinshū* was originally written—which can be deduced from its oldest manuscripts and from early extant fragments of kana poetry—encourages and facilitates the use of puns. Cursive kana, with its lack of a written distinction between voiced and unvoiced sounds, is particularly suited to punning. Unlike most medieval manuscripts of the *Kokinshū*, which tend to feature a liberal use of Sinographs, early man-uscripts are written almost entirely in cursive kana, with only occasional use of Sinographs.

Early *kakekotoba* tend to feature place-names or are puns that constitute the pivot between an introductory preface phrase and the main statement of the poem. Famous mid-ninth-century poets, such as Narihira, Komachi, or Henjō, use puns to create multilayered senses in their poems, often juxtaposing objects that are seen and heard with feelings. A good example by Henjō contains a pun on *omohikurashi* (lamenting all day long) and *higurashi* (cicada):

今こむといひてわかれしあしたよりおもひくらしのねをの
みそなく

"I will come soon" / he said before he left / on that morning, /
and now from dawn to dusk / I cry with the cicadas
(*KKS* 771)

The following poem by Sosei is another good illustration of the kind of punning possibilities of which *Kokinshū* poems take advantage:

をとにのみきくのしらつゆよるはおきてひるは思ひにあへ
すけぬへし

>Hearing rumors / of white dew on chrysanthemums / falling awake /
>
>all night and all day hoping / to perish in the sunlight
>
>(*KKS* 470)

This poem features four puns: *kiku* (hear, chrysanthemums), *okite* (fall, awake), *omohi* (feelings, thoughts) and *hi* (sun), and *kenu* (melt, perish). As is evident from my translation, the full complexity of the puns is impossible to render in English. All a translator can do is make explicit the multiple senses of the words that are designed to be implicit in the puns. One can attempt, however, to reproduce the effect of double-layering created by the puns in the original, and that is what I have tried to do with this translation and in this book.

A related conventional poetic technique is *engo* ("associative words"), which refers to the use of linked images as an extended metaphor. Engo almost always involve the use of one or more puns—in one example of this technique by Tsurayuki, the word *ito* (threads) is associated with *yori* (entwine), *midaru* (come apart) and *hokorobu* (a pun on "blossom" and "unravel"), thereby creating an extended visual conceit between the green willow and a robe:

あをやきのいとよりかくる春しもそみたれて花のほころひ
にける

> The green willow, / its threads entwined together / until
the spring, /

> when the seams are unraveled / by the blossoming flowers
(*KKS* 26)

Engo are often used to superimpose a scene of natural imag-
ery upon the feelings of the speaker, as in the following
example by Ariwara no Motokata, in which the word *nagisa*
(shore) is associated with *nami* (waves), *ura* (beach), and *kaheri*
(return). The poem also contains two puns that link the image
of the waves returning to the beach with the speakers' feelings:
nagisa (shore) and *naki* (not, never), and *urami* (reproach) and
ura (beach):

逢事のなきさにしよる浪なれはうらみてのみそたちかへり
ける

> Just like the waves / are drawn to the shore where /
we never meet, /

> I gaze upon the beach / in reproach as I return (*KKS* 626)

This kind of multilayered, multilinear structure, to borrow
Komatsu Hideo's terms, is often used to create a deliberate sense
of ambiguity that is characteristic of the *Kokinshū* as a whole.
Although there are some straightforward poems in the anthol-
ogy, most compositions—particularly those by the compilers—
appear to be consciously designed to challenge their readers to
make sense of them. What first appear to be straightforward

statements, on closer examination turn out to be deliberately equivocal or contain implicit questions. And a great many poems take the explicit form of questions—although exactly what is being questioned is often less obvious than might at first appear. The organization and sequencing of the *Kokinshū* adds to this challenge, as poems are often arranged strategically to question, echo, respond to, or even contradict each other. This use of equivocation as a rhetorical strategy, both in the poems and in their arrangement in the anthology, makes the *Kokinshū* an ideal object of exegesis.

NOTES

1. In his treatise *Uta no shiki* (*Styles of Poetry*, 772), Fujiwara no Hamanari made an early attempt to articulate rules forbidding the use of the same sound at the end of certain waka measures, by drawing an analogy to the way certain patterns of end-rhyme were regarded as compositional faults in classical Sinitic poetry. Hamanari's ideas do not seem to have gained much acceptance, in part because waka do not actually end-rhyme like Sinitic poetry and also because waka poets did use sound repetition to create auditory effects distinct to specific poems.

2. This difference is evident from the meaning of the Japanese translation of enjambment, *ku-matagari*, literally "line straddling" (which is what the French *enjambment* means). *Ku-matagari* describes a phenomenon in Japanese poetry whereby either a single word or a word and the particle that follows it are split across two measures. Most instances of this occur in the work of modern tanka poets, but examples also appear in Edo-period haikai.

Chapter Six

THE *KOKINSHŪ* PREFACES

COMMENTARY on the *Kokinshū* begins with its two prefaces, traditionally known as the Mana Preface and the Kana Preface.[1] Although often referred to in English as "the Chinese preface" and "the Japanese preface,"[2] these appellations are both inaccurate and misleading. The Mana Preface is a Sinographic text written in a highly accomplished orthodox cosmopolitan style of Literary Sinitic, in a manner and style similar to the prefaces of anthologies of Sinitic poetry compiled both in Japan and China. The Kana Preface is a text written in cursive kana script that represents a stylistically innovative register of vernacular prose writing. The orthodox form of Literary Sinitic was the prestige form of writing par excellence. Cursive kana, by contrast, was a style used in informal contexts, with the sole exception of the writing of vernacular poetry, which was a recent development. The asymmetrical relationship between the two *Kokinshū* prefaces is evident from the fact that even after the compilation of the *Kokinshū*, mana prefaces continued to be written for waka collections as well as for anthologies of Sinitic poetry, whereas kana prefaces were only ever appropriate for waka.

In the tradition of Sinitic poetry that informs the *Kokinshū*, the preface was a literary genre in itself. For instance, the *Wen Xuan* includes "prefaces" (序) as one of its thirty-nine genres of literary writing, with a total of nine entries, arranged in order of prestige and antiquity. These include book prefaces, such as the "Great Preface" to the Mao recension of the *Classic of Poetry* (hereafter, the Mao Preface),[3] the preface to the "old script" text of the *Book of Documents* (*Shangshu*),[4] or Du Yu's (222–284) preface to *Zuo Zhuan*, as well as prefaces to poems or poetic sequences, such as the "Preface to the Three Capitals Rhapsody" by Huangfu Mi (215–282). With the exception of the first entry, the Mao Preface, which was probably composed in the first decades of the Later Han dynasty (25–220 CE), all of the other prefaces included in the *Wen Xuan* date from the third century CE or later. This reflects the fact that the preface developed as a literary genre between the third and sixth centuries, when literature was first conceptualized as an independent bibliographical category. It was from the early Tang dynasty (618–907) onward, however, that the preface became a truly popular form of literary composition. This is as much true of book prefaces, as is evident from the classified encyclopedia *Yiwen Leiju*'s (624) inclusion of a category of "Literary Collection Prefaces" (集序), which begins with Xiao Tong's preface to the *Wen Xuan*, as it is of occasional poetry prefaces, exemplified by the early Tang canonization of Wang Xizhi's *Preface to the Orchid Pavilion* (*Lantingji Xu*, 353) as a calligraphic model.

Just as the Mao recension of the *Classic of Poetry* became the foundational text of Sinitic poetry, its Great Preface came to serve as the canonical preface to the entire poetic tradition, and thus it was always implicitly or explicitly echoed in subsequent prefaces. Because the Great Preface is also the preface to the first poem in the *Classic of Poetry* (all subsequent prefaces to poems are "minor prefaces"), it begins with a statement that describes the first poem ("Fishhawks cry") as representative of the entire genre of "Airs" and indeed of the entire collection:

> "Fishhawks cry" is the virtuous power of the queen consort and the beginning of the Airs (*feng*). It is the means by which all under heaven are influenced and husbands and wives are corrected. It is thus used among village folk and is used in noble states. "Air" means "to influence," it means "to teach." Through the Airs they are moved, through teachings they are transformed.

This is followed by the main section of the preface, which defines what poetry is, how it works, and what its uses are:

> Poems are the outcome of sentiments. Within the mind they are sentiments, expressed in language they become poems. Feelings stir within and take shape as language; when language is not enough, they are cried out in sighs; when crying out in sighs is not enough, they are chanted in song; when chanting in song is not enough, unconsciously the hands begin to move and the feet to dance.

Emotions are expressed in voice. When voice becomes patterned, they are called tones. A well-ordered reign has tones that are peaceful and joyful: its government is in harmony. A chaotic reign has tones that are resentful and angry: its government is in discord. When a state is about to fall, its tones are mournful and pensive: its people are in distress.

Indeed, to judge success and failure, to move heaven and earth, and to affect the spirits and gods, there is nothing that comes close to poetry. The former kings used it to regulate relations between husbands and wives, to inculcate filial obedience and respect, to attend to human relations, to embellish transformative teachings, and to influence manners and customs.

There are six principles of poetry. The first is called "Airs" or Suasion; the second is called Exposition; the third is called Comparison; the fourth is called Evocation; the fifth is called Elegance; the sixth is called Panegyric.[5]

The passage begins with a reformulation of an even older definition of poetry from the *Classic of Documents*, which is attributed to the sage king Shun: "Poetry is the language of sentiment, and song is the chanting of [that] language."[6] The term I translate here as "sentiment" (*zhi*, J. *shi* 志) is more commonly rendered in English as "intent" or "intention."[7] In most cases the graph 志 does indeed mean "intent" in the sense of "aim" or "purpose," but in this context in the Mao Preface, it indicates the mind's reaction to an external circumstance.[8] This reaction gives rise to "feelings" that require expression—people are moved by their circumstances to express their feelings in poetic language, just as they are moved to speak, sigh, sing, or dance. Moreover, as a patterned form of language, poetry itself has the power to move others. An implicit assumption of the preface is that people's minds can be read through their poetry and indeed that poetry can serve as a window into the morals and politics of an age. In sum, the Mao Preface is a foundational statement regarding the radically affective power of poetry as a special kind of patterned chanted speech, and the usefulness to the state of that power when properly regulated.

Note that the relationships among poetry, morality, and politics outlined in the Mao Preface are described as a function of the patterning of voice, speech, and song, with no mention of writing at all. This changed with the development of literary writing as a bibliographical category from the third century onward, when prefaces emerged as a literary genre together with other discursive forms such as treatises and letters.[9] Literary prefaces composed during this period look back on the *Classic of Poetry* and the Mao Preface as canonical texts, but at the same time, they reframe the ideal of poetry as the supreme form of governance within a calligraphic tradition in which writing and script have become the main metaphors for the relationships among poetry, personhood, and good government.

This is the context in which the literary preface was adopted in Japan from the mid-eighth century onward as a genre integral to the practice of Sinitic literary writing. The earliest extant anthology of Sinitic poetry compiled in Japan, the *Kaifūsō*, has a preface, as do all three of the early Heian Sinitic poetry collections, the *Ryōunshū*, *Bunka shūreishū*, and *Keikokushū*. Each of these draws on the language and arguments of renown prefaces and writings on literature from the classical and medieval Sinitic tradition—the *Kaifūsō* on Xiao Tong's preface to the *Wen Xuan* and Ban Gu's preface to the "Rhapsody of Two Capitals," and the three Heian anthologies on Cao Pi's (187–226) essay "Discourse on Literature" (*Lunwen*, J. *Ronbun*), as well as on Liu Xie's (465–522) *The Literary Mind and the Carving of Dragons* (*Wenxin Diaolong*, J. *Bunshin chōryū*), and other texts.

These prefaces make an argument for the utility of literary composition to the state, and in some cases, they also provide a historical narrative of the Sinitic poetry tradition within which to situate the collection they are introducing. In both of these tasks, they make liberal use of the language and arguments of previous canonical models. For instance, the *Kaifūsō* preface articulates a history of literary writing that draws on Ban Gu's preface to the "Rhapsody of Two Capitals" and the *Wen Xuan* Preface, but it transposes their arguments to the genealogical context of the Japanese court. The *Ryōunshū* and *Bunka shūreishū* prefaces are both fairly short and draw on Cao Pi's "Discourse on Literature" to compare Saga's court to the poets of Cao Pi's Jian'an circle and make an argument for the cultural preeminence of "our age." The *Keikokushū*, being a much larger collection, has a lengthier preface that situates the anthology within a history of Sinitic poetry that begins in ancient times but falls into decline during the later Han dynasty. It then goes through a period of renewal in the reign of Cao Pi—to which the reigns of Saga and Junna are again compared—before declining again throughout the Six Dynasties period, and experiencing another revival in the present, at which point the preface studiously avoids mentioning the Tang dynasty and instead foregrounds the accomplishments collected in the *Keikokushū.*

Like their medieval Sinitic models, these prefaces describe poems as individual works that are the physical traces of the artistic craft of literary writing. For instance, the *Kaifūsō* preface refers to "well-wrought writings and beautiful brushwork" and the *Bunka shūreishū* preface refers to "the crafting of writing."[10] The value of such "well-wrought" written works is that they can be transmitted in physical form throughout the ages as traces of the people who authored them. The *Keikokushū* preface thus notes that "the spirit of peace and tranquility once found in the gardens of the Prince of Liang [referring to Xiao Tong, compiler of the *Wen Xuan*] now resides in the fine glory of the poet's brush," and echoes Liu Xie's *Wenxin Diaolong* when it refers to "the authors of antiquity who entrusted their bodies to brush and ink" to achieve literary immortality.[11] Sinitic poems are conceived as artifacts created by brush and paper to be collected and preserved for future readers, in the hope that, in the concluding words of Wang Xizhi's *Preface to the Orchid Pavilion Collection,* "those who hold them in later ages will also be moved by these writings." The literary ideal of Sinitic poetry is thus grounded in a post-third century cultural environment with an established calligraphic tradition in which poems are composed, collected, and transmitted as written works and literary writing exists as an established bibliographical category.

The *Kokinshū* inherits this long tradition of prefaces to anthologies of Sinitic poetry in both China and Japan.[12] The relationship of the literary preface to the tradition of vernacular Japanese song, however, is rather different. Given that the

Man'yōshū has no preface[13]—a curious omission for such a large work, which may reflect the fact that it was compiled through a gradual process of accretion throughout the eighth century— the writers of the *Kokinshū* prefaces were faced with the unprecedented task of introducing not simply an anthology they had compiled but also the entire tradition of vernacular Japanese song. For this reason, although the prefaces to the Heian Sinitic poetry anthologies measure themselves against the well-established Sinitic tradition of literary writing that had developed since the third century, the prefaces to the *Kokinshū* reach further back to model themselves directly on the Mao Preface and draw on its arguments for the universality of poetry as a form of "song." The openings of both *Kokinshū* prefaces follow the Mao Preface's description of poems emerging from the mind to take form in language, but they dress it up in arboreal metaphors:

Waka take root in the ground of the mind and open their blossoms in the forest of words (Mana Preface)

The songs of Yamato take as their seed the human mind and flourish as myriad leaves of words (Kana Preface)

This kind of botanical imagery had become commonplace in the Sinitic literary tradition from the third century onward to describe poetry as a written genre. For instance, the "Rhapsody on Literature" (文賦) by Lu Ji (261–303) famously compares the "substance" of a poem to the trunk of a tree, and its writing to the branches and leaves. Other precedents for botanical tropes can be found in the *Wen Xuan* preface, in which Xiao Tong notes that "during spare moments from my duties supervising the state and tending the army, I have spent much leisure time reading through the garden of letters, extensively perusing the forest of words," and claims that his objective in the process of selection has been to "omit the weeds, and collect the blossoms."[14] A more recent precedent to the *Kokinshū* prefaces can be found in a section of Bai Juyi's "Letter to Yuan Zhen" dated to 815, and collected in volume 28 ("Letters and Prefaces") of *The Bai Juyi Literary Collection* (*Hakushi monjū* 白氏文集):

Literary patterns [writing] are ancient indeed. The three realms each have their patterns: heavenly patterns begin with the three lights [sun, moon, stars], earthly patterns begin with the five elements [fire, water, wood, metal, and earth], and human patterns begin with the six classics. And as for the six classics, they begin with the *Poetry*. They are the reason the sages influenced the minds of the people and thereby brought peace to all under heaven. To influence the minds of the people nothing surpasses emotion, nothing comes before language, nothing approaches voice, and nothing goes deeper than meaning. *In poetry, emotion is the roots, language the branches, voice the blossoms, and meaning the fruits* [my emphasis]. From the sages above to the foolish below, from lowly swine and fish to hidden spirits and gods, the types may vary but the sentiments are the same, the forms may differ but the emotion is one.[15]

The passage begins with a claim that also can be found in the preface of the *Wen Xuan*: just as the heavens and earth have their elemental patterns, writing constitutes the patterns of the human world, and poetry as the most exemplary form of writing represents the epitome of human order. The sequence of "emotion—language—voice—meaning" is a variation on the Mao Preface's description of how poetry moves from "feelings" and "emotions" within the mind into language and voice, but it is dressed up using Lu Ji's metaphor of the trunk, branches, and leaves of a tree. This introduces Bai Juyi's (rather conventional) claim that poetic composition has been declining and losing efficacy since the times of the *Classic of Poetry*, because poets have lost sight of the "six principles" (enumerated in the Mao Preface), and that most compositions consist of superficial poems with beautiful lines but little in the way of deeper meaning, in other words, poems with no "fruit."

Like the Mao Preface, as well as more recent and less canonical texts, such as Bai Juyi's "Letter to Yuan Zhen," both of the *Kokinshū* prefaces link their claims for the universal efficacy of poetry to the six principles. In the Mana Preface, these are cited verbatim immediately following a paraphrase of the Mao Preface's statement on how poetry exerts influence:

> There is nothing that is more suited than waka to move heaven and earth, affect demons and spirits, transform human conduct, and harmonize husband and wife.
>
> There are six principles of waka. The first is called Persuasion; the second is called Exposition; the third is called Comparison; the fourth is called Evocation; the fifth is called Cultivation; the sixth is called Eulogy.

The Kana Preface arranges its argument somewhat differently. After an initial statement on the universal influence of waka, it interposes its account of the mythical and royal origins of song, before stating, "There are six forms of song. It appears that this is also the case with the songs of Kara (China)," and then cites examples of waka poems that exemplify each of the forms. Judging by their names, these "six forms" (suggestive, expository, figurative, comparative, forthright, and panegyric) are clearly intended to be vernacular equivalents of the six principles, even though they do not correspond in every case. The waka chosen to exemplify each "form" have mystified commentators from very early on, beginning with the so-called old notes that appear in all extant manuscripts of the Kana Preface, which conclude by noting "in general it does not really seem possible to divide [waka] into six types." For this reason, most commentators and scholars have tended to regard the citation of the six principles in the *Kokinshū* prefaces as a mostly formal rhetorical gesture toward the Mao Preface whose purpose is to legitimize the *Kokinshū* and waka poetry as comparable to the great tradition of Sinitic poetry. This is understandable given that, as noted earlier, the canonical commentaries to the Mao Preface also have difficulty making sense of the original six principles. I suggest, however, that the obligatory citation of the six principles is in fact quite meaningful and indeed essential to the broader argument of the *Kokinshū* prefaces. In the "Letter to Yuan Zhen," the targets of Bai Juyi's criticism are poets who "hum about the wind and snow and croon about blossoms and plants," but they neglect the six principles by failing to imbue their beautiful imagery with any deeper meaning.

Bai Juyi never discusses what each of the principles represents, but rather seems to use the six principles to signify depth of meaning. Although the exact significance or applicability of each of the six principles may be obscure, what is clear is that they all concern *how* poems express meaning (through various types of comparison or analogy, or directly) and that the significance of the principles as a whole is that, beginning with the first principle of "Airs" or "Suasion," they represent the means through which poetry affects people and transforms their conduct. It is in this light that we should understand the narrative of waka's decline outlined in both of the *Kokinshū* prefaces. Just as in Bai Juyi's letter to Yuan Zhen, the mention of the six principles (or six forms) in the *Kokinshū* prefaces plays a key function in the context of an argument about the need to make waka efficacious once again—as it was once upon a time in the past.

The *Kokinshū* prefaces draw upon the tradition of Sinitic poetic discourse to articulate the close relationship between poetry and imperial authority as well as the function of poetry as the cultural memory of the imperial aristocracy—that is, as literary objects that are preserved to be read by future generations. At the same time, both prefaces make a case for the special significance of vernacular poetry in Japan. According to the Mana Preface, the names of famous waka poets live on in memory because "their words are close to the ears of the people, and their sense accords with the understanding of the gods." In other words, they write in the vernacular, and waka is linked to the imperial divine lineage. In effect, the prefaces argue that in the realm of Japan it is vernacular poems that represent the true "airs" through which the divinely sanctioned sovereign's realm is influenced and transformed.

Both *Kokinshū* prefaces establish the autochthonous lineage of waka poetry first of all by locating its origin in the age of the gods with Susano-o's song "in thirty-one letters," included in both the *Nihon shoki* and the *Kojiki*. The Mana Preface also notes a second mythical point of origin with mentions of a song by the sea-goddess' daughter Toyotama-hime (the paternal grandmother of the legendary first emperor Jinmu) and of imperial compositions by Emperor Nintoku and Prince Shōtoku, who represent the origins of the Japanese traditions of the two main forms of knowledge that came to Japan from the continent, the "outer" and "inner" traditions of Confucian and Buddhist learning, respectively. The implicit argument of the prefaces is that just as poetry is fundamental to all literate knowledge in the realm of Han (as Bai Juyi notes in his "Letter to Yuan Zhen," "the six classics begin with the *Poetry*"), waka occupies a similar foundational role in Japan.

Just as Sinitic literary criticism elevated certain poets of the past as "sages"—as foundational authors of the poetic tradition—the *Kokinshū* prefaces do the same for waka: The Kana Preface refers to Hitomaro as "the sage of song" and in the Mana Preface both Hitomaro and Akahito are called "the sages of waka."[16] As such, Hitomaro represents an ideal time in the past when poetry was the most elevated form of communication between the sovereign and his loyal ministers, and, in the words of the Kana Preface, "sovereign and subject were united as one." Both of the prefaces represent the *Kokinshū* as a return to this ideal time, by drawing an implicit parallel between the "Nara emperor" of ancient times and the present sovereign, Emperor Daigo, as well as, more discreetly, between Hitomaro and the main compiler Tsurayuki.

In the Sinitic tradition, poetry occupies an ambiguous position as the epitome of formal literary writing. On the one hand, literary embellishment provides an elegant form and majesty to the writings of the state. But on the other, it can do this to an excessive degree and can degenerate into frivolity, self-indulgence, and licentiousness. Poetry is revered as the craft of persuasion, but it also is mistrusted for its capacity to lead people astray. This contrast is often articulated in gendered terms: between the kind of poetry deemed appropriate for male court officials—such as they might learn from studying the *Wen Xuan*, and the more "frivolous and alluring"[17] poetry that one might find in the *Yutai Xinyong* (玉台新詠), an anthology that is believed to have been compiled for female readership.[18] This contrast between a stately, principled poetry for male court officials and more licentious, superficial songs for female entertainment also structures the accounts that begin to appear during the Sui and early Tang dynasties. These accounts describe the preceding centuries as a period in which poetry declined because of excessive emphasis on rhetorical ornamentation and overly sensuous expression and subject matter, and argue for the revival of a straightforward, older style of poetry with more substance and depth.

The preface to the *Keikokushū* alludes to this narrative briefly, but in general, we do not find such fears or admonitions regarding the dangers of poetry degenerating into frivolity in any of the Heian Sinitic poetry anthologies. The reason for this is simple: Sinitic poetry at the Japanese court was an elite courtly practice that did not have any connection to popular vernacular lyrics and songs. The *Kokinshū* prefaces, by contrast, inherit these concerns and fears from the tradition of Sinitic poetry in China. Indeed, if waka's advantage over Sinitic poems is that they are "close to the ears of the people" and therefore can influence them, the same quality also makes them prone to degenerate into "trivial compositions."

The *Kokinshū* prefaces thus adopt the Sui-Tang conventional narrative of poetic decline from meaningful poetry to superficial frivolity.[19] For instance, the Mana Preface notes that "the songs of high antiquity" used simple diction, "did not yet indulge in playfulness of the ear or the eye," and served primarily for moral instruction, before they began to decline:

> But then the times turned shallow and people began to admire sensuality. Frivolous words arose like clouds and currents of charm bubbled up like hot springs. All the fruit was fallen and only the blossoms were in bloom. In the houses of the amorous, waka were treated as flowery and flighty go-betweens, and even beggarly monks used them to make a living. And thus it was that they became mostly a method to entertain womenfolk, and inappropriate to present before court officials.

In a similar passage, the Kana Preface notes:

> The world today is attached to colors, and since people's feelings have become like blossoms, all we see are trivial songs and fleeting words; just like trees that are buried in

the garden of amorous pleasures and remain unknown, they do not emerge upright like pampas grass in their proper place.

What the Mana Preface calls "playfulness of the ear and eye" is celebrated as a powerful suasive technique, but without an awareness of these "principles," poetry becomes shallow, "all the fruit was fallen and only the blossoms were in bloom"—mellifluous sounds but without much substance or significance. Or, in the words of the Kana Preface, "since people's feelings have become like blossoms, all we see are trivial songs and fleeting words." The actual examples of each of the six forms in the Kana Preface are all poems with a clear import, and they are meant to contrast with "trivial songs and fleeting words."

It is in this context, too, that we should understand the *Kokinshū* prefaces' discussion and appraisal of the six poets "from recent reigns." They all are acknowledged to be excellent poets who nevertheless do not quite achieve a true understanding of "the meaning of poetry." For the most part, the critiques focus on imbalances between expression and content: Henjō's poetry achieves a good form but lacks substance; Narihira's poems are all emotion and not enough expression; Funya no Yasuhide's poems have skillful diction but their subject matter is inelegant.[20] But they also address deficiencies: the monk Kisen's expression is indistinct, and Ōtomo no Kuronushi's diction is vulgar. The only woman among the six, Ono no Komachi, is characterized as "too sensitive and lacking in strength . . . perhaps because she is a woman" in the Kana Preface and as "having charm but no vitality, like a sick woman wearing make-up," in the Mana Preface.

The description of Komachi's poetry as "charming" (*en* 艶)—a term associated with romantic, sensuous poetry and anthologies like *Yutai Xinyong*—recalls the earlier passage in the Mana Preface regarding the time when poetry became shallow and superficial with "frivolous words arising like clouds and currents of charm (*enryū* 艶流) bubbling up like hot springs," a time when "all the fruit was fallen and only the blossoms were in bloom," and poetry became "mostly a method to entertain womenfolk, and inappropriate to present before court officials." The implication is clear: women's poetry is frivolous by nature and lacks the kind of depth and substance appropriate to the world of male officialdom.

The *Kokinshū* prefaces then present the *Kokinshū* as pointing toward an ideal vision of the future in which waka are no longer limited to the informal medium of amorous correspondence—in the words of the Kana Preface, "like trees that are buried in the garden of amorous pleasures"—but rather feature at formal occasions presided over by the sovereign, "emerg[ing] upright like pampas grass in their proper place." This ideal is one in which the main protagonists of the anthology are male court officials (like the four compilers), and women poets feature only in marginal roles. There is, however, something rather disingenuous about this argument. Skill in composing Sinitic poetry was highly indicative of literate skill in general and therefore of bureaucratic aptitude—as exemplified by the case of Sugawara no Michizane, the famous poet-scholar who rose through the court bureaucracy to reach the position of Minister of the Right. Waka poetry, by contrast, was never regarded as the epitome of bureaucratic literacy, and being an excellent waka poet was of relatively little help in rising through the bureaucracy, as is evident from the low ranks of all four of the *Kokinshū* compilers. Moreover, the formal world of waka banquets and contests that had emerged in the late eighth century and made the compilation of the *Kokinshū* possible was sustained by the practice of waka in the informal contexts of correspondence between members of the aristocracy. Indeed, many of the older poems in the seasonal volumes are love poems featuring seasonal imagery that have been repurposed and recontextualized. The inclusion of such poems has the effect of imbuing the seasonal volumes with implicit or allegorical suggestions of love affairs in the background that at times suggest the sexual politics of the court, which is most evident in the "maiden flower" (*wominahesi*) sequences at the end of the first autumn volume. One way to think of this is that although the "charming" blossoms of love poetry can be taken as representative of political marginal figures, such as Ariwara no Narihira, they could also yield significant fruits in the form of politically advantageous marriages.

Another reason not to take the disavowal of amorous poetry in the *Kokinshū* prefaces at face value is that the anthology contains five volumes of love poetry, which together contain more love poems (359) than the total of the six seasonal volumes (342). When the Mana Preface adopts a common trope of Sinitic poetry to complain that waka have become "mostly a method to entertain womenfolk, and inappropriate to present before court gentlemen," or the Kana Preface makes a point of complaining about "trivial songs and fleeting words," both are studiously ignoring the reality that it was precisely in the context of informal collections of amorous correspondence that cursive kana poetry had developed in the few decades before the compilation of the *Kokinshū*. This is also evident in the fact that the two major figures of mid-eighth century waka included in the *Kokinshū*, Narihira and Komachi, are composers mostly of love poems. In short, without "trivial" love poetry, there would be very little "ancient" in the *Kokinshū* at all.

Given the considerable overlap in content between the mana and Kana Preface s of the *Kokinshū*, the question of which was composed first and the relationship between them has long been a matter of debate. Both prefaces seem to be written in Tsurayuki's voice, but later sources attribute the writing of the Mana Preface to Tsurayuki's distant relative Ki no Yoshimochi (d. 919), son of the renowned Sinitic scholar and politician Ki no Haseo (845–912).[21] Both prefaces mention the date of 905, but in the Mana Preface, this is the date of the preface, whereas in the Kana Preface, it is the date of Daigo's command that the *Kokinshū* be presented to him. In his treatise *Fukurozōshi* (袋草紙, ca. 1157), the waka poet and scholar Fujiwara no Kiyosuke (1104–1177) summarizes two competing theories: one claims that the Mana Preface was written first as a draft on which Tsurayuki later based the Kana Preface, and the other that Ki no Yoshimochi was moved to compose the Mana Preface after reading Tsurayuki's Kana Preface.[22] Given that Tsurayuki is known to have made multiple copies of the *Kokinshū* in his own hand and that all extant manuscripts of the *Kokinshū* include poems from a poetry contest in 913, eight years after the date of 905 given in both its prefaces, it is more than likely that drafts of the two prefaces were compared and rewritten or revised in multiple stages. Notably, in the *Fukurozōshi* account, however, both Kiyosuke and the anonymous authors of the theories he cites seem to assume without question that the Mana Preface was either an early draft or a later addition, and that the Kana Preface was the main preface of the *Kokinshū*.

Textual evidence from both extant *Kokinshū* manuscripts and descriptions of no-longer extant manuscripts in late Heian and medieval texts provide a compelling reason for why the Kana Preface was believed to be more important: very few of the extant complete *Kokinshū* manuscripts include the Mana Preface at all, and those that do almost always include it at the end of the anthology as an appendix, sometimes with notes indicating that they have added the Mana Preface to a copy of a received manuscript that did not include it.[23] Although the earliest of these complete manuscripts dates from the early twelfth century, more than two centuries after the compilation of the *Kokinshū*, their treatment of the Mana Preface is consistent with medieval accounts of original *Kokinshū* manuscripts. In *Fukurozōshi*, Kiyosuke describes "Three Authentic Texts" (*sanshōbon* 三証本) of the *Kokinshū*, two in Tsurayuki's own hand, and the other copied by his sister (or, according to a different source, his wife). Of these three originals, two included only the Kana Preface, and the third, the one that reportedly was presented to Emperor Daigo, did not include a preface at all. Kiyosuke notes that two of these texts had been lost in fires and suggests that the whereabouts of the third was unknown, so these descriptions are not based on his observations, but they do suggest that the Mana Preface was rarely (if at all) included with the *Kokinshū* anthology and that it may have been transmitted separately.

A further indication of the relative status of the two prefaces is the fact that in most extant manuscripts, the Kana Preface contains intralinear glosses—the so-called old notes (*kochū* 古注)—believed to have been written by Fujiwara no Kintō (966–1041) roughly a century or so after the compilation of the *Kokinshū*. Extant manuscripts of the Mana Preface, by contrast, do not have intralinear glosses.[24] There is strong evidence, however, that Kintō held the Mana Preface in high regard, particularly given that the *Wakan rōeishū* (*Collection of Japanese and Chinese Compositions for Chanting*), whose compilation is attributed to Kintō, includes a long citation from the Mana Preface, and that Kenjō's (1130–1209) commentary *Kokinshūchū* (古今集注, 1185) cites numerous annotations by Kintō that clearly refer to the Mana Preface.

What is unquestionable is that by the mid-twelfth century—the date of the earliest extant manuscript—it was the Kana Preface that had become the main object of interest and commentary, and so it would remain throughout the anthology's long history. For this reason, most Japanese scholarly editions put the Kana Preface first, as the more historically significant document, to serve as an introduction to the anthology, and place the Mana Preface in the position of an appendix.[25] In this book, however, I have reversed this practice. In part, I chose to do this simply to highlight the oft-neglected Mana Preface, but also because I believe this order to be a better representation of the status of the two prefaces at the time of compilation. Given that the Mana Preface was written in the official register of Literary Sinitic, that Literary Sinitic prefaces were an established genre, and that previous poetry anthologies compiled during the Heian period also featured prefaces in Literary Sinitic,[26] the reason that the *Kokinshū* has a mana preface is surely because it was believed to be essential at a time before the Kana Preface and the *Kokinshū* anthology had become canonical. Notably, the only other imperial anthology to include both a mana preface and a kana preface, the *Shinkokinshū* (1205), which was compiled long after kana prefaces had become an established literary genre, still places its mana preface first, with the title of "Shinkokinwakashū Preface" (新古今和歌集序) and the kana preface appears second with no title. Another reason for placing the Mana Preface first in this book is that it does a better job at introducing the *Kokinshū*, whereas a full understanding of the Kana Preface requires some previous familiarity with the poetry of the anthology, and in this sense, it reads better as a "postface."

The prefaces are written in different literary registers and therefore fulfill different functions as distinct kinds of literary performance. The Mana Preface is a highly accomplished performance of Literary Sinitic prose, written in a terse discursive style, that describes waka in explicit contrast to Sinitic poetry while simultaneously anchoring it within the lineage of Literary Sinitic writing. At times, the Mana Preface places waka within the Sinitic tradition without comment, such as when it lists the "six principles of waka" that are identical to the "six principles" of the Mao Preface to the *Classic of Poetry*. In a similar manner as a preface to a Japanese anthology of Sinitic poetry, the Mana Preface also superimposes local features onto the preexisting Sinitic cultural landscape, as in one of its closing lines: "Ah, Hitomaro may be gone, but are waka not here with us?," which is a simple rephrasing of the well-known line from the *Analects*, "King Wen may be gone, but is *wen* (culture) not here with us?"[27] Through this technique of superimposition, Hitomaro is reaffirmed as the founding cultural figure and "sage of waka." The Mana Preface thus takes full advantage of the way in which the cultural authority of Literary Sinitic is closely tied to canonical texts and figures from the Sinitic tradition, to make an argument for the prestige of waka poetry. It also does this to compare waka favorably to Sinitic poetry: for instance, the statement, "when the letters of that House of Han [Sinitic writing] were transmitted, the customs of our sun-region [the realm of Japan] were transformed; the endeavors of the people were completely changed, and waka began to gradually decline," echoes conventional narratives of "decline of the kingly way" (*ōdō otorohe* 王道衰) that derive from the Mao Preface and many other Sinitic texts, to blame the decline of waka on the ascendance of Sinitic poetry in Japan.

The Kana Preface is written in a style that in many ways resembles a vernacular "reading by gloss" (*kundoku*) of Literary Sinitic. It would not take much effort, for instance, to rewrite the second sentence in the Kana Preface in Literary Sinitic: "The people who live in this world, in their abundant concerns and affairs, relate the thoughts in their minds to the things they see and hear, and so express them." At the same time, in contrast to the Mana Prefaces's terse, economic style of Literary Sinitic, the Kana Preface tends toward expansive and circumlocutionary turns of phrase that make frequent use of the aspectual auxiliary verb *keri*, in a manner that is uncharacteristic of the vernacular gloss reading of Literary Sinitic but very typical of the form of kana vernacular fiction known as *monogatari*.

The Kana Preface rarely alludes explicitly to Sinitic precedent—the only real instance is the remark after introducing the six forms of song that "it seems this is also the case with the poetry of Kara," and strives to embody the fantasy of a non-Sinitic vernacular literary space. It does so, however, within the broader realm of Sinographic writing: Sinitic literary authority is always present in the background, just as the "native" written style of cursive kana derives its prestige from the Sinitic tradition of cursive calligraphy.

What the Kana Preface is able to do is "perform" the poetry anthology in a way that the Mana Preface cannot, because it shares a common written register with the poems in the anthology. In its account of how "the sovereigns of the reigns of old" would command their attendants to compose poetry, the Kana Preface presents a long sequence of allusions to poems included in the various volumes of the *Kokinshū*. There is no counterpart to this extended section in the Mana Preface, although as Timothy Wixted has noted, one can find similar passages in Sinitic treatises about Sinitic poetry,[28] because unlike the Kana Preface, the Mana Preface does not inhabit the same written register as the waka poems collected in the anthology.

Unlike kana vernacular fiction, in which citations from poems often blend with and are incorporated into prose, the Kana Preface generally distinguishes itself as vernacular prose from poetry by avoiding verbatim phrasings from waka, even when alluding to specific poems, and it also tends to avoid using puns. Occasionally, however, it does make use of punning to incorporate the kind of multilayered patterns of *Kokinshū*-style poetry. As Komatsu Hideo has argued,[29] it does so in its opening lines, in which the phrase "myriad leaves" (*yorodu no koto no ha*) hints at a pun in the preceding phrase "the human mind" (*hito no kokoro*), whereby the word *hito* can be read as both "human" and "one/single," thus rendering the following multilayered sentence:

The songs of Yamato take a single/human mind as their seed and flourish as myriad leaves of words.

やまとうたは、ひとのこころをたねとして、よろつのことのは とそなれりける.

In its opening, the Kana Preface thus presents the cursive kana script of waka as the medium for the multilayered possibilities of reading that characterize the *Kokinshū*. Note that the multilayered punning that the Heian cursive kana script makes possible is not simply or even primarily an oral phenomenon. Words such as *kiku*, meaning both "hear" (聞) and "chrysanthemum" (菊), or *okite*, meaning both "awaking" (起) and "falling" (置), are oral puns, but many poetic puns in the *Kokinshū* are ambiguous only in written form and rely on the exclusion of the use of full-form Sinographs and the deliberate lack of a distinction between voiced and unvoiced sounds.[30] Typical examples of this are ひくらし to represent both *hikurashi* (日暮らし, evening falling) and *higurashi* (蜩, cicada), or なかれて for both *nakarete* (泣かれて, weeping) and *nagarete* (流れて, flowing). In other words, it is the conventions of cursive kana script that make the multilayered expression of *Kokinshū* poetry possible.

When the Mana Preface defines waka as "a composition in thirty-one letters" first recited by Susano-o, or the Kana Preface notes that "songs . . . since the time of the god Susa-no-o have been composed in thirty letters and one," "letters" is referring both to written symbols and to the patterning of sound into syllables. This is an ambiguity that is also present in the classical Sinitic sense of the term *wen* or *bun* (文) meaning "pattern" (both written and aural), as well as the Shingon Buddhist idea of "letters" (*ji*, 字) as a distinct unit of sound, which influenced the formation of the kana syllabaries. When Tsurayuki notes at the end of the Kana Preface that "though the seasons may pass, things may be lost, and joy and sadness come and go, the letters of these songs will be here," the "letters" (*moji*, もじ) of waka that will remain for posterity refer to the cursive kana script, and he is claiming that the cultural authority of waka from now on will be closely tied to the authority of cursive kana as an aristocratic form of vernacular writing.

NOTES

1. Note that no extant manuscript of the *Kokinshū* includes these titles. Manuscripts that include the Mana Preface title it simply as the "*Kokin-wakashū* Preface." Conversely, the Kana Preface is always left untitled in manuscripts of the *Kokinshū* anthology, although a twelfth-century stand-alone manuscript of the Kana Preface also titles it as the "*Kokin-wakashū* Preface." To my knowledge, there are no extant examples of the prefaces being distinguished by the titles of Kana Preface and Mana Preface before the twelfth century, although they probably were referred to informally by these titles.

2. See, among others, Laurel Rasplica Rodd, *Kokinshū: A Collection of Poems Ancient and Modern* (Princeton, NJ: Princeton University Press, 1984; repr., Cheng & Tsui, 1996); Helen McCullough, *Kokin Wakashu: The First Imperial Anthology of Japanese Poetry* (Stanford, CA: Stanford University Press, 1985); and Timothy Wixted, "The *Kokinshū* Prefaces:

Another Perspective," *Harvard Journal of Asiatic Studies* 43, no. 1 (June 1983): 215–238.

3. Traditionally attributed to Confucius' disciple Zixia (fl. fifth century BCE), but more realistically to Wei Hong (first century CE).

4. Attributed to Kong Anguo (ca. 176–74 BCE), but probably a forgery dating from the Wei or Jin dynasties.

5. See *Maoshi zhengyi. Shisanjing zhushu*, vol. 4 (Beijing: Beijing daxue chubanshe, 2000), 11–12. Complete English translations of the Great Preface can be found in Michael Fuller, *An Introduction to Chinese Poetry* (Cambridge, MA: Harvard University Asia Center, 2018), 51–52.

6. *Shangshu zhengyi. Shisanjing zhushu*, vols. 2–3 (Beijing: Beijing daxue chubanshe, 2000), 95.

7. Other translations are "earnest thought" (James Legge), "aim" (Steven Van Zoeren), or "resolve" (Michael Fuller).

8. Hence Stephen Owen's rendering as "what is intently on the mind." Stephen Owen, "The Courtly Yongwu," in *The Poetry of the Early Tang* (New Haven, CT: Yale University Press, 1977; repr., Melbourne: Quirin Press, 2012), 45-55.

9. See Christopher M. B. Nugent, "Literary Media: Writing and Orality," in *The Oxford Handbook of Classical Chinese Literature (1000 BCE-900 CE)*, ed. Wiebke Denecke, Wai-Yee Li, and Xiaofei Tian (Oxford: Oxford University Press, 2017), 46–60.

10. See *Kaifūsō, Bunka shūreishū, Honchō Monzui, Nihon koten bungaku taikei* 69, ed. Takagi Ichinosuke et al. (Tokyo: Iwanami shoten), 60 and 193.

11. See *Keikokushū, Kōchū Nihon bungaku taikei* 24, ed. Saku Misao (Tokyo: Seibundō, 1933), 234

12. Prefaces would become even more popular in the two centuries after the compilation of the *Kokinshū*. The mid-eleventh-century collection of Japanese Sinitic literature *Honchō Monzui* (*Literary Masterpieces of This Court*, ca. 1060), which modeled its organization on the *Wen Xuan*, includes the staggering number of one hundred and fifty-six prefaces (six book prefaces, 139 Sinitic poetry prefaces, and eleven waka poetry prefaces). See Saeko Shibayama, *Ōe no Masafusa and the Convergence of the "Ways": The Twilight of Early Chinese Literary Studies and the Rise of Waka Studies in the Long Twelfth Century in Japan* (PhD diss., Columbia University, 2012), 63.

13. The *Man'yōshū* does include eight prefaces to poems and poem sequences written in the tradition of occasional Literary Sinitic prefaces. Seven of these are in volume 5 and one is in volume 17.

14. See *Monzen: Shihen* 6, ed. Kawai Kōzō et al. (Tokyo: Iwanami shoten, 2019), 416–438.

15. *Hakushi Monjū* 5, *Shinshaku kanbun taikei*, vol. 101, 347.

16. Similar descriptions can be found in Sinitic texts such as Zhong Rong's (465–518) *Gradings of Poems* (詩品, *Shipin*, J. *Shihin*), in which the Jian'an era poets Cao Zhi (192–232) and Liu Zhen (d. 217) are called "the sages of literature."

17. See Xiaofei Tian's discussion of *Yutai Xinyong* in *Beacon Fire and Shooting Star: The Literary Culture of the Liang* (Cambridge, MA: Harvard Asia Center, 2007), 107–109, 174–195.

18. Both of these texts were well-known in Japan. The *Wen Xuan* is mentioned in the Taihō code of 701 as text that all (male) students at the imperial academy should consult after the classics. *Yutai xinyong* was not a canonical text like *Wen Xuan*, but it was well known to the *Kokinshū* compilers. It is included in Fujiwara no Sukeyo's (847–897) comprehensive *Catalogue of Books in the State of Japan* (*Nihonkoku kenzaisho mokuroku*), compiled between 875 and 891, and evidence from the *Man'yōshū* strongly suggests that it was available in Japan since at least the first half of the eighth century.

19. In addition to Bai Juyi's account of poetic decline in his "Letter to Yuan Zhen," another well-known version of this narrative in Japan was that of Wang Changling (698–757) in his "Discussion of the Meaning of Literature," which was collected in *The Secret Archive of the Mirror of Letters* (*Bunkyōhifuron* 文鏡秘府論, 819–820), a collection of selected literary criticism by various Chinese authors compiled by Kūkai. For an English translation, see Richard W. Bodman, *Poetics and Prosody in Early Mediaeval China: A Study and Translation of Kūkai's Bunkyō Hifuron* (Melbourne: Quirin Press, 2020).

20. Sinitic precedents for such appraisals of famous poets can be found in Cao Pi's *Lunwen*, in which he discusses the strengths and weaknesses of each of the Seven Masters of the Jian'an reign: "Ying Yang is pleasant but lacks vigor; Liu Zhen is vigorous but lacks reserve. Kong Rong's form and spirit are lofty and subtle . . . but . . . his principle does not match his diction."

21. The Mana Preface is attributed to Yoshimochi in *Honchō monzui* (*Literary Masterpieces of This Court*, ca. 1060) and is included as the first of eleven waka prefaces written in Literary Sinitic. This attribution seems to have been followed by the extant *Kokinshū* manuscripts that include

the Mana Preface, all of which date from the twelfth century or later. It is clear, however, that the first-person voice of the Mana Preface belongs to Tsurayuki, and that Yoshimochi's role, as a scholar of Sinitic learning who was not well-known for his waka poetry (he has a single composition in the *Kokinshū*), was that of a proxy writer.

22. See *Fukurozōshi*, vol. 1, *Shin Nihon koten bungaku taikei* 29, ed. Fujioka Tadaharu (Tokyo: Iwanami shoten, 1995), 53. For a summary of views and debates on this issue in modern scholarship, see Katagiri Yōichi, *Kokin-wakashū zenhyōshaku*, vol. 1 (Tokyo: Kōdansha, 1998), 89–92.

23. The oldest extant manuscript to include both mana and kana prefaces is the so-called Jien text, which was discovered in 2010, dates from the early Kamakura period, and is a copy of one of Teika's early transcriptions.

24. See Nishimura Kayoko, "*Kokinshū* kanajo 'kochū' no seiritsu," *Chūko bungaku* 56 (1995):10–18.

25. This is the case with the *Shin Nihon koten bungaku taikei* edition that is the basis for this English translation, as well as the *Shinpen Nihon koten bungaku zenshū* edition (Tokyo: Shōgakukan, 1994), and Takeoka Masao's *Kokinshū zenhyōshaku* (Tokyo: Yūbun shoin, 1976). The two complete translations of *Kokinshū* into English by Rodd and McCullough 1985 also follow this order. Katagiri Yōichi's relatively more recent *Kokinshū zenhyōshaku* (Tokyo: Kōdansha, 1998) places both at the beginning, with the Kana Preface first, followed by the Mana Preface.

26. Mana prefaces are appended not only to the three imperially commissioned anthologies of Sinitic poetry in the early eighth century, but also the two late-eighth-century anthologies that included both Sinitic poetry and waka: the *Shinsen Man'yōshū* and *Kudai waka* (*Chisato shū*).

27. "Ah, Hitomaro may be gone, but are waka not here with us?" (嗟乎、人丸既沒、和歌不在斯哉); see *Analects* (9.5): "King Wen may be gone, but is wen (culture) not here with us?" (文王既沒、文不在茲乎).

28. Wixted suggests that the Kana Preface's list of allusions is modeled on a similar passage in Zhong Rong's (468–518) *Poetry Gradings* (*Shi Pin* 詩品), also known as *Poetry Critiques* (*Shi Ping* 詩評). See Wixted, "The *Kokinshū* Prefaces," 215–238.

29. See Komatsu, *Miso hito moji no jojōshi: Kokin wakashū no waka hyōgen wo tokihogusu* (Tokyo: Kasama shoin, 2004), 93–94.

30. I say deliberate, because as Komatsu Hideo points out, the full-form phonographs in the *Man'yōshū* do distinguish between voiced and unvoiced sounds.

Chapter Seven

THE *KOKINSHŪ* TEXT AND ITS COMMENTARIAL TRADITION

NOT LONG after its completion, the success and popularity[1] of the *Kokinshū* led to the establishment by Emperor Murakami (926–967, r. 946–967) in 951 of a Waka Bureau in the quarters of his empress consort. Staffed by five notable scholars known as "the Pear Courtyard Five," the bureau worked on two main projects: the production of cursive kana script glosses of the *Man'yōshū*, and the compilation of a second imperial anthology, the *Gosenwakashū*, or *Collection of Later Selections of Japanese Poetry* (951). The name of this second anthology, the fact that its compilers did not include any of their own compositions, and the focus on poems by the *Kokinshū* compilers and their contemporaries in the Engi era (901–923) all suggest that its purpose was to be a sequel to the *Kokinshū*. The third imperial collection, *Shūiwakashū* or *Collection of Gleanings of Japanese Poetry* (ca. 1005), also includes many compositions by the compilers of the *Kokinshū*, as well as a substantial number of *Man'yōshū* poems that were retranscribed into cursive kana script. Both the *Gosenshū* and the *Shūishū* include a far greater number of poems by members of the highest ranks of the aristocracy than their predecessor, which indicates that the *Kokinshū* prefaces' stated aim of raising the status of waka poetry at court indeed was successful. By the beginning of the eleventh century, the *Kokinshū* had become the foundational text of a waka tradition dedicated to the cultural continuity of the imperial court.

The canonical status of the *Kokinshū* is illustrated by a famous episode in Sei Shōnagon's *Pillow Book* (ca. late tenth century), in which Sei's mistress Empress Teishi (977–1001) recounts a story about Emperor Murakami, who having heard that his consort Hōshi (d. 967)[2] had memorized the entire *Kokinshū* decides to test her over two entire nights, at the end of which Hōshi is able to completely recite the anthology without a single mistake. This story has probably been embellished, but it is Teishi's subsequent self-deprecatory comment after marveling at Hōshi's feat that "I don't think I could manage more than the first few volumes," which emphasizes the degree to which the study of the *Kokinshū* was central to court life. The fact that Murasaki Shikibu's *Tale of Genji* (early eleventh century) contains more than two hundred and fifty references and citations to poems in the *Kokinshū* is another clear indication that substantial familiarity with the anthology was assumed as a given.

In the late tenth and eleventh centuries, conventions began to be established at poetry contests regarding the proper ways to compose waka on set "topics" (*dai*) according to poetic precedent. The compilation of the fourth imperial anthology, *Goshūishū* or *Collection of Later Gleanings* (1088), which was fiercely critiqued by a rival of the main compiler, marks a key moment when poetry contests and the compilation of imperial anthologies became the object of intense competition over poetic expertise within the court.[3] This rivalry coincides with the conceptualization of poetry as a "way" and an object of study, the development of different factions claiming expertise in poetry and the beginning of a competitive tradition of waka commentary and exegesis that was primarily focused on the *Kokinshū*. It is from this context that specialized poetic lineages emerged among the twelfth-century aristocracy, "who devoted themselves to the production, preservation, and transmission from generation to generation of knowledge of poetic composition, criticism, and precedent."[4] The first of these lineages was the Rokujō House, founded by Fujiwara Akisue (1055–1123), and perhaps best represented by Akisue's grandson Kiyosuke (1104–1177) and his adopted grandson Kenjō (also known as Kenshō, 1130–1210). Their rival the Mikohidari House was founded by Fujiwara no Shunzei (1114–1204) and his son Teika (1162–1241). The differences between the two lineages are perhaps best represented by the debate between Kenjō and Shunzei over appropriate uses of diction and sources in the *Poetry Contest in Six Hundred Rounds* (*Roppyakuban uta awase*) held in 1193. As Thomas McAuley has described, Kenjō aimed to revitalize waka by reaching beyond the *Kokinshū* back to the *Man'yōshū* as a source of unusual diction and rhetoric, whereas Shunzei was more concerned with cultivating a circumscribed and elegant diction based on the *Kokinshū* and promoting styles of poetry that appeared to be simple yet were deeply moving.[5] Of the two schools, the Mikohidari House was more successful—first with the appointment of Shunzei as sole compiler for the *Senzaishū* or *Collection for One Thousand Years* (1188), and then with the compilation of the eighth imperial anthology, *Shinkokinshū*, or *New Ancient and Modern Collection* (1205) by a team of six that included one member of the Rokujō House but otherwise was monopolized by the Mikohidari, led by Shunzei's son Teika. As its title indicates, the *Shinkokinshū* paid homage to the *Kokinshū* while simultaneously setting a new standard for poetic composition that would influence an additional thirteen imperial anthologies compiled from the thirteenth to the mid-fifteenth centuries.

In this way, the *Kokinshū* was recanonized as the foundational anthology of the courtly tradition of vernacular poetry—a text to be interpreted and reinterpreted in each successive age. The earliest annotated commentaries on the *Kokinshū* appear in the twelfth century—examples of these are Fujiwara no Norinaga's *Kokinshū Notes* (1177), Kenjō's *Kokinshū Notes* (1183), and Shunzei's *Kokin Question and Answer* (1191)—and proliferate thereafter: some three hundred commentaries on the *Kokinshū* were produced between the twelfth and the nineteenth centuries.[6] No other poetry anthology comes even close to this number, and the only other vernacular classical texts that can even compare are *Tales of Ise* and the *Tale of Genji*. The attitude toward the *Kokinshū* is succinctly summarized by Shunzei's exhortation in his treatise *Poetic Styles from the Past* (*Korai fūteishō*, 1197): "for the fundamental forms of poetry, one should look up to the *Kokinshū*."[7]

Once the *Kokinshū* was established as the foundation of poetic knowledge and practice, the possession, preservation, and transmission of reputable manuscripts became crucial to its readerly exegesis and to any claims to poetic expertise. It is for this reason that from the mid-twelfth century onward different poetic houses and factions begin to produce their own manuscript lineages of the *Kokinshū*, based on authenticated copies of originals reputed to have been in Tsurayuki's own hand. In *Fukurozōshi* (1157), Rokujō poet Kiyosuke describes "Three Authentic Texts"[8] of the *Kokinshū*. The first he refers to as "The Empress Dowager Yōmeimon'in Book" (陽明門院御本). Yōmeimon'in was a title of Princess Teishi (1013–1094), consort of Emperor Go-Suzaku (r. 1036–1045). Kiyosuke notes that this was the original "Engi Book" (延喜本), that is, the text that was presented to Emperor Daigo. It was in Tsurayuki's hand, had no prefaces, and was lost in a fire. The second text is known as "The Ono Empress Dowager Book" (小野皇太后宮御本), after a title of Fujiwara no Kanshi (1021–1102), Empress to Go-Reizei (r. 1045–1068). This text was also written in Tsurayuki's hand, included the Kana Preface, and was originally presented to Daigo's Empress Consort Onshi (885–954). The third text is known as "The Hanazono Minister of the Left Book" (花園左府御), after Minamoto no Arihito (1103–1147), included the Kana Preface, and was penned by a younger sister of Tsurayuki (other sources have this as Tsurayuki's wife, or as Tsurayuki himself). This text purportedly belonged to "the Kan'in Great Minister," also known as Fujiwara no Kinsue (957–1029). Kiyosuke notes that this text was presented (by Arihito?) to the "New Retired Emperor," that is, Retired Emperor Sutoku (1119–1164, r. 1123–1142).[9]

Although partial fragments of the *Kokinshū* manuscripts survive that date from the mid-eleventh century, the oldest extant complete manuscripts date from more than two centuries after the *Kokinshū* was compiled: the Gen'ei text (元永本) of 1120[10] and the "Attributed to Kintō" manuscript (伝公任筆本), which has been dated to the mid-twelfth century and was discovered in the early 1990s. The Masatsune manuscript (雅経本; mid- to late twelfth century) is believed to be a copy made by Asukai Masatsune's (1170–1221) (one of the six compilers of *Shinkokinshū*) of a manuscript by Fujiwara no Norinaga (1109–1180), which was in turn based on a personal copy of Tsurayuki that belonged to Emperor Sutoku (1119–1164, r. 1123–1142).[11]

In addition to these three manuscripts, there are three textual lineages, named after three of the major poets and scholars of the late Heian and early Kamakura periods: Kiyosuke, Shunzei, and Teika. The Kiyosuke texts (清輔本) survive in the form of several thirteenth-century second-hand transcriptions (i.e., copies of copies) of mid- to late-twelfth-century manuscripts written in Kiyosuke's hand. Kiyosuke is known to have copied the *Kokinshū* multiple times, in almost all cases basing his copy on a manuscript by Fujiwara no Michimune (1040?–1084), which was in turn a copy of the manuscript presented by Tsurayuki to Daigo's Empress Consort Onshi (885–954), known as "The Ono Empress Dowager Book." Kiyosuke created his own manuscript lineage by comparing the Onshi manuscript with the Sutoku manuscript. Shunzei's texts (俊成本; mid- to late twelfth century) were edited by comparing the Sutoku manuscript with a different manuscript by Fujiwara no Mototoshi (1060–1142). The Teika texts (定家本) are by far the most numerous, with Teika having copied the *Kokinshū* at least seventeen times, of which eleven survive, two in his own hand, and nine transcriptions. Teika based his work on one of Shunzei's texts (the *Shōwagire*), which survives only partially, and made emendations based on other manuscripts. The Teika texts are the basis of almost all modern editions of the *Kokinshū*.[12]

It would be hard to overstate Teika's influence on the subsequent reception of the *Kokinshū* and indeed on the waka tradition as a whole. Teika wrote several commentaries of *Kokinshū*, among them *Kenchū mikkan* (*Secret Observations on Kenjō's Commentary*, 1221), an annotated version of Kenjō's *Kokinshū Notes* of 1183 in which he critically absorbed much of Kenjō's learning into the Mikohidari tradition of *Kokinshū* exegesis. Teika was succeeded by his son Tameie (1198–1275), who dedicated himself to continuing his father's legacy. After Tameie's death, his children quarreled over his estate and the Mikohidari house split into three rival houses named after the location of their residences in the Heian capital—the Nijō, founded by Fujiwara no Tameuji (1222–86); the Kyōgoku, founded by Fujiwara no Tamenori (1227–79); and the Reizei, by Fujiwara no Tamesuke (1263–1328).[13] Throughout the late thirteenth and fourteenth centuries, these houses vied with each other over property disputes and claims to authority, competed for imperial favor and the privilege of editing imperial anthologies, and sought out contacts and allegiances with the warrior class, who were eager to learn waka composition and acquire its cultural prestige. Of these, the Nijō school was the more influential and most successful at securing imperial patronage: Nijō poets served as compilers for seven imperial anthologies between 1278 and 1384, versus only two by the Kyōgoku school, and none by the Reizei. These poetic lineages, as well as others such as the Asukai, all produced numerous commentaries on the *Kokinshū*. In addition to philological commentary, each of the poetic houses developed their own "secret teachings" of the *Kokinshū* that claimed to uncover hidden allegorical meanings in the text, often relating waka to esoteric Buddhist teachings.[14] Although early modern and modern scholars lambasted these allegorical interpretations as bizarre and far-fetched, a different way to read them is as sociohistorical adaptations of the claim that poetry has special efficacy. In a broader sense, they are consistent with Shunzei's claim that "poetry has led people the way to the Buddha,"[15] and with the medieval notion that Japanese songs or waka, like Indian dharani and Sinitic poetry, possess a transcendent power.[16] Through these allegorical interpretations the *Kokinshū* became a source for Nō plays and for the late-medieval narrative genre known as *otogi zōshi*.

By the fifteenth century, the imperial sponsorship of poetry anthologies had effectively ended—its last project was the *Shinshoku kokinwakashū* of 1439, which was in fact sponsored by an initiative of the Ashikaga shogunate. With the exception of the Reizei, the poetic houses had become extinct and their knowledge had been inherited by nonaristocrats: a number of prominent poets and authorities on the *Kokinshū* in this period were monks of the midranking warrior class and other commoners of even humbler status. In this context, a group of poets who had received their teachings from poets affiliated with the Nijō and (to a far lesser extent) the Reizei schools revived the tradition of "Secret Teachings of the *Kokinshū*" (*kokin denjū*). Men such as Sōgi (1421–1502) and Jōen (1401?–1484?) were no longer aristocrats seeking patronage—the imperial court was impoverished—but commoners who made a living from poetry by charging tuition. As was the case with the earlier secret transmissions in the Kamakura period, their commentaries had two layers of meaning: a "surface" interpretation and an "underlying" or secret teaching. An example of this is *Ryōdō no kikigaki* (*Two Readings*, 1472), a transcription by Sōgi (1421–1502) of Tō no Tsuneyori's (1405?–1484?) lectures on the *Kokinshū*. The allegorical readings of this revived tradition of secret teachings were less concerned with esoteric Buddhist meanings as they were with relating the poems of the *Kokinshū* to neo-Confucian principles of harmonious government and ethical action, as befitted the interests of their age. It was Sōgi who initiated the aristocrat Sanjōnishi Sanekata in the *Kokinshū* Secret Teachings, which were then transmitted within the imperial court up to the twentieth century.[17]

A key turning point in the history of *Kokinshū* commentary was the development of commercial woodblock printing in the mid-seventeenth century. The *Kokinshū* was printed in 1682 and circulated widely as part of the poet and scholar Kitamura Kigin's (1625–1705) printed *Annotations on the Hachidaishū* (八代集抄). Modern scholars divide *Kokinshū* commentaries into old and new, beginning with Keichū's *Ancient and Modern Leftover Timber Commentary*[18] or *Kokin yozaishō* of 1692. As Lewis Cook has noted, in the context of printed book culture, which defines knowledge "as a commodity available for accumulation and distribution in exchange for other commodities or hard currency," literary commentary that is "published" (as opposed to circulating through copies of manuscripts that are transmitted from master to disciple) makes its disagreements with other commentary public.[19] In such a context, the main way for a new commentary to attract readers and establish itself as an authority is by prefacing its own interpretations with polemical critiques of earlier commentaries. This emphasis on proposing a correct reading of a poem that supersedes earlier interpretations is different from the medieval tradition in which commentaries did not compete in the form of commercially available published books, but rather were transmitted within poetic lineages or only to those who were admitted into the poetic tradition, and debates over the meaning of a poem took place within a restricted social milieu of poet-scholars representing the interests of their poetic lineage. One way of thinking about this difference between medieval and early modern commentary is that the latter are selling a compelling argument for a single correct interpretation, whereas the former are offering multiple readings. This is not simply a case of distinguishing between two different levels of "surface" philological readings and "hidden" allegorical interpretations, but rather is an acknowledgement within the philological commentary that many poems appear to yield more than one plausible reading, suggesting that it may be necessary to entertain more than one reading simultaneously. The fact that early modern and modern commentaries were often highly critical of medieval allegorical exegesis has obscured the reality that, as Cook has observed, few new readings of *Kokinshū* poems have been proposed after the fifteenth century and early modern and modern commentaries rely far more heavily on medieval exegesis than their polemical critiques might suggest. In a sense, the medieval style of commentary is better suited to a collection such as the *Kokinshū*—whose poems often deliberately equivocate between different senses and playfully encourage misreadings—than the self-avowedly more rational or positivistic early modern and modern commentaries.

Throughout the momentous sociopolitical and cultural changes from the seventeenth to the nineteenth centuries, the *Kokinshū* continued to be revered as the foundational classic of waka poetry. A key turning point came in the late nineteenth century, with the emergence of modern national literary histories. The tanka and haiku poet Masaoka Shiki (1867–1902) is famous for his polemical attack on the *Kokinshū* in the second of his "Letters to Uta Poets." Published in 1898, it opens with the provocative statement, "Tsurayuki is an inept poet and the *Kokinshū* is a worthless anthology," and goes on to critique the entire collection as being "full of hackneyed puns and sophistry."[20] Shiki's critique was in large part determined by his belief in the literary value of what he called "true depiction" and describing the world "as it is." He disapproved of the *Kokinshū* tendency toward verbal artifice and fanciful conceits (such as birds "crying" tears) and recommended aspiring poets read the *Man'yōshū* for what he regarded as its more authentic expressions of emotion. This was not an entirely original argument— Shiki apparently was not all that familiar with the *Man'yōshū* when he wrote his "Letters to Uta Poets" and appears to have been relying on early modern scholarship. Literary historians subsequently marked Shiki's anti-*Kokinshū* polemic as a key moment in a reversal of fortunes whereby the *Kokinshū* was displaced as the foundational poetic anthology of the vernacular literary tradition. In a context in which this tradition was no longer conceived in hierarchical terms as the cultural property of the aristocracy, which nonaristocrats had come to share, but rather as a fundamental property of the people, the *Man'yōshū*—as the older, larger, and more socially diverse anthology—could more plausibly represent the entire nation than the undisguisedly aristocratic *Kokinshū*.[21]

In practice, however, the *Kokinshū* continued to be studied extensively, particularly in an academic context. It bears emphasizing that more than ninety commentaries on the *Kokinshū* and countless pieces of academic scholarship were published during the twentieth century, and more work continues to be published in the twenty-first, not only on the *Kokinshū* but also on the long history of its reception, and not only in Japanese but also in many other languages, including English. Today, as in the past, the *Kokinshū* continues to be the essential point of entry into the study of classical and medieval aristocratic literature.

NOTES

1. Gian Piero Persiani refers to this as the "boom of waka poetry in the mid-tenth century." See Persiani, *Waka After the Kokinshū* (PhD diss., Columbia University, 2013).
2. Daughter of Fujiwara no Morotada (920–969), who was promoted to Minister of the Right in 967 and Minister of the Left in 969.
3. See Robert N. Huey, "The Medievalization of Poetic Practice," *Harvard Journal of Asiatic Studies* 50, no. 2 (December 1990): 651–668. See also Ariel Stilerman, "Cultural Knowledge and Professional Training in the Poetic Treatises of Late Heian Japan," *Monumenta Nipponica* 72, no. 2 (2017): 153–187.

4. See Anne Commons, "Japanese Poetic Thought, from Earliest Times to the Thirteenth Century," in *The Cambridge History of Japanese Literature*, ed. Haruo Shirane, Tomi Suzuki, and David Lurie (Cambridge: Cambridge University Press, 2015), 224.

5. See Thomas McAuley, *The Poetry Contest in Six Hundred Rounds: A Translation and Commentary*, 2 vols. (Leiden: Brill, 2020), 28–39.

6. The *Shin Nihon koten bungaku taikei* edition of the *Kokinshū* (published in 1989) lists 297 commentaries. The earliest of these dates from the beginning of the twelfth century, which has fifteen commentaries in total. Seventeen more commentaries were written in the thirteenth century, more than thirty in the fourteenth, more than twenty-five in the fifteenth, twenty-seven in the sixteenth, twenty-two in the seventeenth, twelve in the eighteenth, forty in the nineteenth, forty in the first half of the twentieth century (before 1945), and fifty in the second half of the twentieth century.

7. "For the fundamental forms of poetry, one should look up to the *Kokinshū*" (歌の本躰には、ただ古今集を仰ぎ信ずべき事なり).

8. Manuscripts certified in a colophon as being authentic copies of one of Tsurayuki´s originals.

9. For a discussion of the "Three Authentic Texts" see Katagiri Yōichi, *Kokin wakashū zenhyōshaku*, vol. 1 (Tokyo: Kōdansha, 1998), 87.

10. Reputedly copied by Minamoto no Toshiyori (aka Shunrai, 1055–1129), but present consensus attributes it to Fujiwara Sadazane (1063–1161). It includes the (untitled) Kana Preface but no Mana Preface. At the time of publication, the Gen'ei text can be fully accessed online at http://www.emuseum.jp/ [in Japanese].

11. Some believe this manuscript is actually in Norinaga's hand, which would date it to the Heian period. See Katagiri, *Kokin zenhyōshaku*, 40–45.

12. See Katagiri, *Kokin zenhyōshaku*, 40–45. For instance, the *Nihon koten bungaku zenshū* edition is based on a copy by Teika's great grandson Nijō Tameyo (1250–1338), which is dated to 1273. Teika's Jōō text (1223) circulated widely and thus exists in the form of multiple different transcriptions, by Teika's son Tameie, and later by his descendants Tamesada and Tameaki in the fourteenth century, some of which were then recopied in the seventeenth century. Some of these transcriptions are the basis of the old and new *Nihon koten bungaku taikei* editions and others. The seventeenth-century woodblock print edition of another transcription is the basis for the *Nihon koten bungaku shūsei* edition. The *Kokka taikan*

edition is based on the Date Masamune (1567–1636) text, which is in Teika's own hand and did not circulate until the twentieth century. Katagiri's *Kokinshū zenhyōshaku* is based on the Karoku text (1226), which is in Teika's hand, and is in the possession of the Reizei family.

13. See Steven D. Carter, "Waka in the Medieval Period: Patterns of Practice and Patronage," in *The Cambridge History of Japanese Literature*, ed. Haruo Shirane, Tomi Suzuki, and David Lurie (Cambridge: Cambridge University Press, 2015), 238–255.

14. See Susan Blakeley Klein, *Allegories of Desire: Esoteric Literary Commentaries of Medieval Japan* (Cambridge, MA: Harvard University Asia Center, 2002).

15. For an English translation of selections from *Korai fūteishō* (*Poetic Styles from the Past*, 1197), see Haruo Shirane, ed., *Traditional Japanese Literature: An Anthology, Beginnings to Sixteen Hundred* (New York: Columbia University Press, 2007), 587–592.

16. This is a claim made most famously in Mujū Ichien's *Shasekishū* (1283). On this topic, see R. Keller Kimbrough, "Reading the Miraculous Powers of Japanese Poetry: Spells, Truth Acts, and a Medieval Buddhist Poetics of the Supernatural," *Japanese Journal of Religious Studies* 32, no. 1 (2005): 1–33.

17. On *Kokin denjū*, see Lewis Cook, *The Discipline of Poetry: Authority and Invention in the Kokindenju* (PhD diss., Cornell University, 2000). See also Cook's brief essay "Waka and Commentary," in *Waka Opening Up to the World: Language, Community, and Gender* (Tokyo: Bensei shuppan, 2012), 350–364, and Unno Keisuke's essay "A History of Reading: Medieval Interpretations of the *Kokin wakashū*," *Waka Opening up to the World*, 340–349.

18. The title of "Leftover Timber" suggests that it is a sequel to Keichū's commentary on the *Man'yōshū*, the *Myriad Ages Substitute Craftsman's Records* or *Man'yō daishōki* (万葉代匠記), where "substitute craftsman" is a conventional self-deprecating description of one's abilities that originates in the *Laozi*.

19. See Cook, *The Discipline of Poetry*, 43.

20. See Shiki, "Futatabi utayomi ni atauru sho," in *Shiki zenshū* 7 (Tokyo: Kōdansha, 1975), 23.

21. See "Jojibun," in *Shiki zenshū* 14 (Tokyo: Kōdansha, 1976), 241–249.

22. See Shinada Yoshikazu, "*Man'yōshū*: The Invention of a National Poetry Anthology," in *Inventing the Classics: Modernity, National Identity, and Japanese Literature* (Stanford, CA: Stanford University Press, 2002), 31–50.

Chapter Eight

TRANSLATING THE *KOKINSHŪ*

FOLLOWING THE STANDARD PRACTICE of regarding Teika's texts as superior to the others (i.e., as having corrected transcription errors and thus presumably likely to be closer to Tsurayuki's originals), for this translation, I have used the *Shin Nihon koten bungaku taikei* edition (hereafter cited as *SNKBT*) of the *Kokinshū*, whose base text is a seventeenth-century transcription of a late-fourteenth-century manuscript by Nijō Tamesada (1293–1360), which was in turn one of several copies of a no longer extant copy of a manuscript written in Fujiwara no Teika's own hand.

One reason that later texts such as Teika's are regarded as being closer to Tsurayuki's original is that the older manuscripts of the *Kokinshū* that date to the Heian period tend to emphasize calligraphic skill. The problem with texts such as the Gen'ei manuscript is that they often contain more copy errors—in part because the copyists were primarily focused on transcribing the calligraphy and may not always have been paying much attention to the sense of the poems, and probably because they were also somewhat unfamiliar with the diction of poems that had been written two centuries earlier. From the mid-twelfth century onward, once waka and the *Kokinshū* became an object of study, the main function of manuscripts was to be an authoritative copy of an older text. They were copied by courtiers who were noted poets and scholars of the *Kokinshū*. The Kiyosuke, Shunzei, and Teika lines of manuscripts are all intent on correcting errors of transcription and striving to preempt the possible miscopying of their own texts. One consequence of this approach is that early Kamakura manuscripts—in particular those by Teika—use Sinographs far more often in the writing of poetry than the manuscripts from the Heian period. This does indeed make the poems easier to copy, and mistakes less likely; at times, however, it also has the effect of removing ambiguity from the poems and of inserting Teika's interpretations of poems into the text. As is the case with many Heian classics, the *Kokinshū* we read today is in many ways a post-Teika anthology.

For this reason, even as I agree with the basic premise of using the Teika lineage of manuscripts as the base text for modern editions, I also share Komatsu Hideo's mistrust of the calligraphic style of the post-Teika *Kokinshū* texts, with their far more liberal use of Sinographs. Thus, to get a sense of what an all—or mostly—kana *Kokinshū* text might have looked like in the tenth century, I also consulted the Gen'ei text on many occasions. Even in cases in which a poem is identical when read aloud in each manuscript, the effect of the two different styles of writing is quite striking, as should be evident by the following comparison between the text of the *SNKBT* edition and a typographic transcription of the Gen'ei manuscript. The following example is by Tsurayuki:

霞たちこのめも春の雪ふれは花なきさとも花そちりける

かすみたちこのめもはるのゆきふれはゝなゝきさともはなそ
ちりける

    The haze rises, / and on budding trees spring / snow is falling, /

    so even blossomless gardens / are now covered in blossoms (*KKS* 9)

The Gen'ei poem is written entirely in kana, whereas the *SNKBT* base text includes four Sinographs that correspond to poetic topoi—haze (霞), spring (春), snow (雪), and blossoms (花).[1] Komatsu suggests that these two forms of writing the poem are, in effect, two different writing systems—one purely cursive kana, the other a Sinograph-cursive kana mix.[2] There is certainly a significant difference between encountering the word *haru* written as (はる) and realizing that it is a pun on the trees "budding" and the season of "spring," and encountering it with the Sinograph for spring (春) as the primary meaning and realizing that a secondary sense of budding or growing (張) is also being suggested. This version has a certain ceremonial elegance, with its sequence of spring motifs written in Sinographs to stand out, particularly when viewed in the context of the first spring volume of the *Kokinshū*: the previous poem uses four Sinographs (spring, day, I, snow), and the following poem uses three (spring, blossoms, warbler). But the poem that Tsurayuki wrote in all likelihood looked more like the Gen'ei manuscript, which allows the reader to vacillate between the two meanings of a pun without necessarily viewing either of them as the primary sense.

Most existing English translations of the *Kokinshū* and other waka include texts of the original poems written in the Roman alphabet in a system of Japanese romanization that reflects their modern pronunciation. This can be convenient for readers (such as myself) who know classical Japanese and want to check the translation quickly against the original without looking the poem up in a proper Japanese edition. It also made a lot of sense in the days when most readers of an English translation of waka poetry did not have immediate access to an original text. In this book, however, I do not include Japanese romanized text alongside the English translations. In part, this is because I would like the translations to stand by themselves. But I also believe the addition of Romanized originals can often have the effect of relegating the translations to the secondary or supplementary role of English-language glosses to a Romanized transcription that is actually quite far from being an original text. I would refer readers who can read Japanese script and know classical Japanese to the online *Kokinshū* text at the Japanese Text Initiative at the University of Virginia, which is based on a manuscript in Teika's hand known as the Date Family Text, and is the basis for the *Shinpen kokka taikan* edition of the *Kokinshū*. Perhaps because it is actually written in Teika's hand and is not a later copy, the ratio of Sinographs to kana is also lower than in other Teika-line manuscripts, and thus it is a good compromise text between the "all-cursive kana" style of the Gen'ei text in which the *Kokinshū* was probably originally written and manuscripts copied at a later time.[3] I also refer readers to the Gen'ei text and to other manuscripts available online.[4]

Broadly speaking, there are two ways to translate waka into English. One is to approximate the prosodic pattern of 5/7/5/7/7, either in the form of alternating short and long lines of varying length, or by strictly replicating the syllabic count in English.[5] The other is to ignore the meter of the original and simply create an English translation in the shape of a poem in short lines (usually five, but not always) with no defined prosodic pattern.[6] The direct reproduction of the syllabic prosodic pattern of waka in English has two major and well-known drawbacks. First, the English translation often has to add words that are not in the original to make up the syllabic count. This tends to create an effect of wordiness that is quite unlike the sparseness of the originals. In this respect, translating waka into poem-like stacks of five short lines with no defined prosodic pattern tends to produce more elegant and accurate translations of individual poems. The second drawback is that the syllable is not a unit of rhythm in the English language, which means not only that the result often does not sound like prosodic language at all but also that unlike the case of Japanese, in which all combinations of five and seven syllables share a rhythmic signature no matter what words they make up, in English the imposing of five- and seven-syllable patterns does not create a common sound pattern shared by all the translations.

My solution has been to translate the prosodic pattern of waka into an English equivalent by creating loose iambic lines from the combination of short and long measures. I attempt to recreate the flowing rhythm of the original by allowing each measure to run on into the next (i.e., I do not try to "end-stop" each measure). This is an example of my translation of the following poem by Tsurayuki:

> That water where
> I drank and drenched my sleeves
> before it froze,
> today that spring has come
> will it melt in the wind? (*KKS* 2)

袖ひちてむすひし水のこほれるを春立けふの風やとくらむ

The first two measures form an iambic pentameter, "That water where / I drank and drenched my sleeves," as indeed do measures 2 and 3, "I drank and drenched my sleeves / before it froze," and 3 and 4, "before it froze, / today that spring has come," with the last two measures beginning with an iambic trimeter, "today that spring has come" and dissolving into a ternary rhythm (an anapestic dimeter) "will it melt in the wind?" I have picked an example of a near-perfect iambic pattern for the purposes of illustration. In many cases, the rhythm of my translations is only loosely iambic, but throughout the book, I have generally adhered to the principle of translating the combination of 5/7 Japanese syllables into an English (once again, loosely) iambic line that divides into 4/6 or 4/7. This results in an English translation that feels rhythmically natural while maintaining (or creating) a prosodic form of five measures in a "short-long-short-long-long" pattern that is common to all the translated poems. To reflect the fact that the "rhythmic period" in a waka poem is not the individual measure but rather the combination of 5/7 measures, I have departed from the conventional practice of indenting the two shorter measures (the first and third),[7] and instead I indent the three longer measures (the second, fourth, and fifth), as a way of formalizing the convention of indenting "run-over" lines.

Unlike previous translations of the *Kokinshū*, which tend to approach the translation of each poem individually as a discrete composition without much regard for the ways in which different poems in the collection echo and relate to each other, my strategy in this book has been to translate the poems as part of a larger meaningful poetic language. The difference can be illustrated by the case of the first poem in the second spring volume (*KKS* 69), whose topic and author are both marked as "unknown." The following comparison features my translation (TD), followed by translations by Helen McCullough (HM), Laurel Rodd (LR), and Edwin Cranston (EC). For reference, I have also provided a transcription of the Gen'ei manuscript, the *SNKBT* text, and a romanized reading.

はるかすみたなひくやまのさくら花うつろはむとやいろか
はりゆく (Gen'ei manuscript)

春霞たなひく山の桜花うつろはむとや色かはり行
(*SNKBT* text)

Cherry blossoms   harukasumi
   in the spring haze that trails   tanabiku yama no
over the hills,   sakurabana
   do they reflect their passing   utsurowamu to ya
   the colors that are fading? (TD)   iro no kawariyuku

   Might they be waiting
to scatter from these branches
   those cherry blossoms
growing ever paler now
in the hills where spring haze trails (HM)

   on distant mountains
where spring mists float and trail
   the cherry blossoms
change color is it to tell
us of their yearly passing (LR)

   The cherry blossoms
Flowering where the mountains drift
   With springtime haze
Are they soon to strew the ground?
Their color has begun to change. (EC)

Except for the fact that McCullough inverts the grammatical order, the sense of the other three translations is fairly similar. All agree, as do I, that the phrase *iro kahariyuku* means "changing color" or "fading" ("growing paler" in McCullough's version). The key to the poem is what the verb *uturofu* means. Its usual meaning is also "to change color," "fade," or "to pass," hence Rodd's translation of it as "yearly passing." Some commentators (including Teika, in his commentary *Kenchū mikkan*) suggest it should be read as synonymous with the verb *tiru*, "to scatter," hence McCullough's translation "to scatter from these branches" and Cranston's "strew the ground."[8] In this case, however, there is a good case to be made for *uturofu* being a pun that also includes the meaning of "shine" or "be reflected," as Sōgi's commentary *Ryōdō no kikigaki* (*Two Readings*) suggests.[9] Indeed, the question "are their colors changing because they are about to fall/scatter?" seems to be somewhat redundant and pointless for a poem in an anthology in which rhetorical questions are almost always playful. In contrast, reading *uturofu* as a pun yields a conceit in which the pale pink color of the spring haze trailing over the hills is imagined to be the reflected tinge of the blossoms, and thereby an allusion to the Sinitic sense of the Sinograph for "haze" (霞), suggesting the rose-pink clouds in the sky at dawn or at dusk. The poet asks if the blossoms are about to fade just as they are being reflected in the skies for a brief moment of glory. In this reading, it is the blossoms that are the subject of both the "fading" and the "reflection." A variation on this reading—which I have tried to convey in my translation—is one in which the poet is deducing that the fading pink-tinged spring haze at dawn over the mountains is in fact due to the reflection of the cherry blossoms.[10] This is a highly plausible interpretation in light of other poems in the second spring volume, in which the reflection (*kage*) of the blossoms is caught in the trailing spring haze:

> The haze of spring
>   looks like a thousand colors
> trailing over
>   the mountains as it catches
>   reflections from the blossoms (*KKS* 102)[11]

春霞色のちくさに見えつるはたなひく山の花のかけかも

My point, however, is not so much to argue for my reading of *KKS* 69,[12] but rather to illustrate that my translation is not simply a rendering of this individual poem, but of the poem as it forms part of the larger whole of the anthology. This becomes even clearer when we look at a poem by Tomonori in the fourth love volume, in which the first three measures of *KKS* 69 reappear in identical form:

春霞たなひく山の桜花みれどもあかぬ君にもある哉

Cherry blossoms	Harukasumi
in the spring haze that trails	tanabiku yama no
over the hills,	sakurabana
just like I look at them	miredomo akanu
I never tire of you (*KKS 684*)	kimi ni mo aru kana

On the surface, this seems like a straightforward poem, expressing the fairly unremarkable sentiment: "I will never tire of you just like I never tire of looking at the beautiful scene of the cherry blossoms through the spring haze on the hills." This is the sense of all three of the following translations by McCullough, Rodd, and Cranston:

> I shall never tire
> of these trysts with a flower
>   fair as the cherries
> on which I gaze unsated
> in the hazy hills of spring (HM)

> I never weary
> of the fragile cherry blooms
>   on the mountain where
> spring mists trail though I often
> gaze upon you I'll not tire (LR)

> Lacings of spring mist
> Drifting on the mountainside
>   Cherry trees in bloom:
> I could gaze at you forever,
> Never wearying of love (EC)

Yet readers of these translations who cannot read the originals would never know or be able to guess that the first three measures of *KKS* 684 are identical to those of *KKS* 69, as a side-by-side comparison of each translator's renderings of the two poems should illustrate:

KKS 684

> I shall never tire
> of these trysts with a flower
>   fair as the cherries
> on which I gaze unsated
> in the hazy hills of spring (HM)

> I never weary
> of the fragile cherry blooms
>   on the mountain where
> spring mists trail   though I
> gaze upon you   I'll not tire (LR)

> Lacings of spring mist
> Drifting on the mountainside
>   Cherry trees in bloom:
> I could gaze at you forever,
> Never wearying of love (EC)

KKS 69

> Might they be waiting
> to scatter from these branches
>   those cherry blossoms
> growing ever paler now
> in the hills where spring haze trails (HM)

>   on distant mountains
> where spring mists float and trail
>   the cherry blossoms
> often change color   is it to tell
> us of their yearly passing (LR)

> The cherry blossoms
> Flowering where the mountains drift
>   With springtime haze
> Are they soon to strew the ground?
> Their color has begun to change. (EC)

Given that *KKS* 684 incorporates three entire measures of the earlier poem, there is no question that it is meant to be read with *KKS* 69 in mind. That is to say, both the pun of "passing/reflecting" and the "colors that are fading" from *KKS* 69 are implicit in (folded into) Tomonori's love poem:

KKS 69

Cherry blossoms
   in the spring haze that trails
over the hills,
    do they reflect their passing
    the colors that are fading?

KKS 684

Cherry blossoms
   in the spring haze that trails
over the hills,
    just like I look at them
    I never tire of you

This pair of poems was chosen by a student in my undergraduate seminar on the *Kokinshū* in response to the exercise prompt, "pick a poem from the love volumes that relates to a poem in the seasonal volumes in an interesting way." The student interpreted *KKS* 684 as saying "even if your colors fade (like the spring haze and cherry blossoms in *KKS* 69), I will never tire of you." Another student proposed a more ironic reading, arguing that while on the surface Tomonori's poem promised to "never tire," it was also playfully hinting that, just as in *KKS* 69, the love affair might last for a brief while before fading. As support for their interpretation, this student referred the class to the following poem from the second spring volume by another of the compilers, Mitsune:

When I look at
   the blossoms, my heart too
starts to change hue;
   I will not show my colors
   lest they betray my thoughts (*KKS* 104)[13]

This prompted a third student to wonder whether the poem could be expressing a shared understanding that love affairs are brief moments of infatuation in which people pledge they will never tire of one another even as they know deep down that this too will fade away, like everything else.

This discussion is just one example among any number of similar debates in which students in my classroom have proposed different readings of a specific poem by searching for similar language and points of reference in other poems. I have my own thoughts about the merits of each of the three interpretations, but what is important to me as a teacher and translator is that they are all plausible readings of the original poems, even though the students had experienced only the English translation. That is what I hope this book accomplishes: to allow English-speaking readers to become immersed in the *Kokinshū* and enjoy reading each poem in relation to other poems by exploring the language and networks of associations that make up the poetic world of the anthology.

NOTES

1. Note that the actual modern editions "translate" Teika's text even further into mixed Sinograph-hiragana text, by supplying additional Sinographs and indicating with furigana those places where Teika's original had kana.
2. See Komatsu Hideo, *Teinei ni yomu koten* (Tokyo: Kasama shoin, 2008).
3. See Japanese Text Initiative, University of Virginia, http://jti.lib.virginia .edu/japanese/kokinshu/index.html [in Japanese]. For instance, *KKS* 9 is written as 霞たちこのめもはるの雪ふれば花なきさとも花ぞちりける, with "haze," "snow," and "blossoms" all written in Sinographs as 霞, 雪, and 花, but with the pun on "budding" and "snow" in kana as はる.

4. The Gen'ei manuscript is available at https://emuseum.nich.go.jp/ [in Japanese]; see 古今和歌集 (元永本).

5. A loose version of this is Robert H. Brower and Earl Miner's *Japanese Court Poetry* (Stanford, CA: Stanford University Press, 1961), which uses alternating short and long phrases of widely varying lengths (often far wordier than the original). Helen McCullough and Laurel Rodd's complete translations of the *Kokinshū* follow a strict syllabic pattern of 5/7/5/7/7. See Laurel Rasplica Rodd, *Kokinshū: A Collection of Poems Ancient and Modern* (Princeton, NJ: Princeton University Press, 1984; repr., Cheng & Tsui, 1996); and Helen McCullough, *Kokin Wakashu: The First Imperial Anthology of Japanese Poetry* (Stanford, CA: Stanford University Press, 1985). Edwin Cranston and Steven Carter both use relatively strict syllabic patterns but with some variation—long lines can be 7/8 syllables, short lines 4/5. See Edwin Cranston, *A Waka Anthology*, vol. 2, *Grasses of Remembrance* (Stanford, CA: Stanford University Press, 2006); and Stephen D. Carter, *How to Read a Japanese Poem* (New York: Columbia University Press, 2019).

6. This is the strategy adopted by Jane Hirschfield in *The Ink Dark Moon: Love Poems by Ono no Komachi and Izumi Shikibu, Women of the Ancient Court of Japan* (New York: Vintage Classics, 1990), by Lewis Cook's translations of the *Kokinshū* in Haruo Shirane's *Traditional Japanese Literature: An Anthology* (New York: Columbia University Press, 2007), or by Thomas McAuley in his *Kokinshū* translations (and translations from many other anthologies) at https://www.wakapoetry.net.

7. Early English translations of waka do not use indentation. For instance, W. G. Aston's *A History of Japanese Literature* (London: 1899), Arthur Waley's *Japanese Poetry: The Uta* (1920), and William N. Porter's translation of *Tosa Diary* (London: H. Frowde, 1912) all use five lines but no indentation. Porter's *A Hundred Verses from Old Japan* (Tokyo: Tuttle, 1909) lineates the romanized transcription by indenting the first and third measures, but in the English translation he indents the second, fourth, and fifth. In French, Bonneau's *Rhythmes Japonais* (1932) indents the first and third lines of both romanized transcription and translation, as do his selections from the *Kokinshū* (1933–1934). The convention of indenting the first and third lines in English seems to have been established by Brower and Miner, *Japanese Court Poetry*.

8. Note also that neither "branches" nor "ground" are in the original—they have been added to make up extra syllables.

9. See Takeoka Masao, *Kokin wakashū zenhyōshaku*, vol. 1 (Tokyo: Yūbun shoin, 1976), 385.
10. This is Motoori Norinaga's (1730–1801) reading of the poem.
11. Keichū brings up this poem in his commentary on *KKS* 69.
12. Which is also that of Sōgi, Keichū, Norinaga, Lewis Cook, and many others before me.
13. 花みれは心さへにそうつりける色にはいてし人もこそしれ.

POETS IN THIS BOOK

MEMBERS OF THE HEIAN NOBILITY belonged to lineage groups called *uji* (氏)—large and loosely affiliated complex clusters of families who shared common ancestry. Some lineage names are derived from hereditary occupations (Ōtomo, Nakatomi, Inbe), others from geographic areas (Ki, Ōshikōchi, Mibu, Sugawara, Ono), and yet others from the emperor's bestowal of a lineage name on a loyal subject (Fujiwara, Taira) or on a prince (Ariwara, Minamoto). All of the poets in the *Kokinshū* were aristocrats who belonged to a lineage. For instance, the name of the main compiler, Ki no Tsurayuki, means "Tsurayuki of the Ki lineage" and the author of the first poem in the anthology, Ariwara no Motokata, is "Motokata of the Ariwara lineage."

The different households within lineages were not all necessarily closely related. For instance, the two "Ki" who compiled the *Kokinshū*, Tsurayuki and Tomonori, were first cousins, but the author of the *Kokinshū* Mana Preface, Ki no Yoshimochi, was a rather distant relation—he was eight generations removed from a common ancestor—and belonged to a far more prominent household: his father was the famous scholar Ki no Haseo, who rose to the third rank. Similarly, the poet Fujiwara no Toshiyuki belonged to the southern branch of the Fujiwara and was not closely related to his contemporary Fujiwara no Tokihira, who was Minister of the Left and belonged to the northern branch.

Abe no Nakamaro 安倍仲麿 **(698–770):** An eighth-century court official who was a member of the 716 embassy to the Tang court, where he remained to serve Emperor Xuanzong (r. 713–756). He went on to take the civil examinations and became a Tang court official, serving as governor of Annam toward the end of his life. He became close friends with Tang poets, including Li Bai (701–762) and Wang Wei (699–759). Author of one poem in the *Kokinshū*.

Archbishop Henjō 遍照僧正 **(816?–890):** His lay name was Yoshimine no Munesada. A grandson of Emperor Kanmu, he served as chamberlain (*kurōdo*) to Emperor Ninmyō, and became a Tendai monk after Ninmyō's death in 850. He studied with the Tendai chief abbot Ennin at Enryakuji, and later with Enchin at Miidera. In 869, he became abbot of Urin Temple and in 877 of Gangyōji, where he took up residence and was appointed archbishop (*sōjō*) in 885. He was also known as the "Archbishop of Kazan" (or "Hanayama" in the vernacular reading of the same graphs), after the name of the area north of the Heian capital where Gangyōji was located. Author of seventeen poems in the *Kokinshū*.

Ariwara no Motokata 在原元方 **(dates unknown):** Narihira's grandson. Author of fourteen poems in the *Kokinshū*.

Ariwara no Muneyana 在原棟梁 **(d. 898):** Narihira's son. Served as palace guard to the crown prince and later governor of Echizen. Author of four poems in the *Kokinshū*.

Ariwara no Narihira 在原業平 **(825–880):** Grandson of Emperor Kanmu (735–806, r. 781–806) on his mother's side, and Emperor Heizei (773–824, r. 806–09) on his father's side. His father, Prince Abo, was exiled to Tsukushi for fourteen years following the Kusuko Incident of 810. Narihira served in the palace guards during the reigns of Ninmyō (808–850, r. 833–850) and Seiwa (850–878, r. 858–876). He also served Emperor Montoku's (826–858, r. 850–58) son Prince Koretaka (844–897). In the reign of Emperor Yōzei (869–949, r. 876–884), he was appointed chamberlain the year before his death in 879. In the *Nihon Sandai Jitsuroku* (*True Records of the Three Reigns* of Japan, 901), he is described as "elegant and handsome of both complexion and appearance, yet dissolute and without restraint (. . .) He had no academic talent, but was skillful at composing waka." He is the author of thirty poems in the *Kokinshū*, all of which are prefaced by extended headnotes and also appear in *Tales of Ise*.

Ariwara no Yukihira 在原行平 **(818–893):** Like his younger brother Narihira, he served the court during the reigns of Ninmyō, Montoku, Seiwa, Yōzei, and Uda, and despite a period of exile to Suma during Montoku's reign, he had a more successful career, reaching the position of middle counselor and the third rank during Yōzei's's reign in 882. The Mana Preface mentions him together with Ono no Takamura as an example of someone who was a talented poet but achieved fame through other means. Author of four poems in the *Kokinshū*.

Emperor Kōkō (830–887, r. 884–887): Son of Emperor Ninmyō. In the *Kokinshū*, he is referred to as the "Ninna Emperor." Author of two poems in the *Kokinshū*.

Former Great Minister of the Realm: *See* Fujiwara no Yoshifusa.

Fujiwara no Kanesuke 藤原兼輔 **(877–933):** Murasaki Shikibu's great-grandfather. He held the posts of chamberlain and middle counselor and rose to the third rank. Author of four poems in the *Kokinshū*.

Fujiwara no Kachion 藤原勝臣 **(dates unknown):** A lower-ranking courtier active during the late ninth century. Author of four poems in the *Kokinshū*.

Fujiwara no Koremoto 藤原惟幹 **(dates unknown):** Author of one poem in the *Kokinshū*.

Fujiwara no Kotonao 藤原言直 **(dates unknown):** A contemporary of the compilers and author of one poem in the *Kokinshū*.

Fujiwara no Kunitsune 藤原国経 **(827?–908):** Older brother of Chancellor Mototsune and Empress Takaiko. He served as major counselor. Author of one poem in the *Kokinshū*.

Fujiwara no Okikaze 藤原興風 **(dates unknown):** A contemporary of the *Kokinshū* compilers, he was reputed to be a talented musician. Author of seventeen poems in the *Kokinshū*.

Fujiwara no Sekio 藤原関雄 **(805–853):** Served at the courts of Junna (786–840, r. 823–833) and Ninmyō (808–850, r. 833–850). Had an unremarkable career as an official but was noted for being a skilled musician, calligrapher, and poet, both of waka and of Sinitic poetry. Two of his poems are included in the *Kokinshū* and one of his compositions appears in *Keikokushū*.

Fujiwara no Sugane 藤原菅根 **(855?–908):** Graduated from the imperial university as doctor of letters and served as chamberlain. Was exiled to Dazaifu in 901 with Sugawara no Michizane. Upon his return, he served at Daigo's court and later contributed to the compilation of *Engi shiki* (*Rules and Procedures of the Engi Era*, 927). Author of one poem in the *Kokinshū*.

Fujiwara no Tadafusa 藤原忠房 **(d. 928):** A midranking official who became governor of Yamashiro. Author of four poems in the *Kokinshū*.

Fujiwara no Tadayuki 藤原忠行 **(d. 906):** A midranking official who served as governor of Wakasa. Author of one poem in the *Kokinshū*.

Fujiwara no Takaiko 藤原高子 **(842–910):** Daughter of Regent Fujiwara no Yoshifusa and sister to Chancellor Fujiwara no Mototsune. She was Emperor Seiwa's Empress Consort, and mother to Emperor Yōzei. In the *Kokinshū*, she is referred to as the "Nijō Empress Consort." Author of one poem in the *Kokinshū*.

Fujiwara no Tokihira 藤原時平 **(871–909):** Son of Chancellor Mototsune. He was appointed Minister of the Left during Daigo's reign in 899. Author of two poems in the *Kokinshū*.

Fujiwara no Toshiyuki 藤原敏行 **(d. 901 or 907):** An official from the highest ranks of the middle aristocracy, he served in a variety of positions that required literary skills. Was renowned as one of the finest calligraphers of his day. Author of nineteen poems in the *Kokinshū*.

Fujiwara no Yoruka 藤原因香 **(dates unknown):** Daughter of Fujiwara Takafuji. Active from the reigns of Seiwa to Daigo. Author of four poems in the *Kokinshū*.

Fujiwara no Yoshifusa 藤原良房 **(804–872):** Author of one poem in the *Kokinshū* and reputed author of another.

Funya no Asayasu 文屋朝康 **(dates unknown):** Yasuhide's son, he was appointed controller of the palace guard in 902. Author of one poem in the *Kokinshū*.

Funya no Yasuhide 文屋康秀 **(dates unknown):** One of the six poets of the recent past discussed in the Mana Preface and Kana Preface, he was a relatively low-ranking official who served in a series of undistinguished positions in the late ninth century. His last appearance in the historical record is in 880. Author of five poems in the *Kokinshū*.

Furu no Imamichi 布留今道 **(dates unknown):** A lower-ranking court official who served during the latter half of the ninth century. Author of three poems in the *Kokinshū*.

Harumichi no Tsuraki 春道列樹 **(d. 920):** A graduate of the imperial university, he was named governor of Iki in 920 but died before taking up his post. Author of three poems in the *Kokinshū*.

Imperial Kinsman Minister of the Right: *See* Minamoto no Yoshiari.

Ise (ca. 872?–ca. 938) Daughter of Fujiwara no Tsugukage, who was governor of Ise ca. 885. She also served as lady in waiting to Empress Onshi and was a concubine of Emperor Uda. Author of twenty-two poems in the *Kokinshū*.

Kakinomoto no Hitomaro 柿本人麿 **(dates unknown, fl. late seventh century):** The greatest poet in the *Man'yōshū* (ca. eighth century), where his name is more properly written as 人麻呂. The Kana Preface to the *Kokinshū* describes him as "the sage of poetry." Seven anonymous poems in the *Kokinshū* are attributed to him in the endnotes, but none of these appear in the *Man'yōshū*, and their attribution to Hitomaro is almost certainly apocryphal.

Kamutsuke no Mineo 上野岑雄 **(dates unknown):** Active during the third decade of the ninth century. Author of one poem in the *Kokinshū*.

Kasa no Shōen 笠勝延 **(827–901):** A priest at Tōdaiji and Enryakuji. Author of one poem in the *Kokinshū*.

Kawara Minister of the Left: *See* Minamoto no Tōru.

Ki no Aritomo 紀有朋 **(d. 880):** Tomonori's father and author of two poems in the *Kokinshū*.

Ki no Aritsune's daughter 紀有常娘: A daughter of the court official Ki no Aritsune (815–877) who was married to Narihira, according to the preface of her only poem in the *Kokinshū*.

Ki no Tomonori 紀友則 **(dates unknown):** One of the four compilers of the *Kokinshū*. Judging by two poems composed after his death by his co-compilers Ki no Tsurayuki (who was also his cousin) and Mibu no Tadamine, he died before the anthology was completed (see poems 838–839). Author of forty-six poems in the *Kokinshū*.

Ki no Toshisada 紀利貞 **(d. 881):** Served in a series of bureaucratic scribal positions. Author of four poems in the *Kokinshū*.

Ki no Tsurayuki 紀貫之 **(872?–945?):** Served the court of Daigo as director of the library (大内記) and various other positions. Was governor of Tosa from 930 to 935. The main compiler of the *Kokinshū* and author of the Kana Preface, he is also the author of 101 poems in the collection.

Ki no Yoshimochi 紀淑望 **(d. 919):** A classical scholar who was the son of the renowned scholar and Middle Counselor Ki no Haseo, and a distant relative of Ki no Tsurayuki. Author of the Mana Preface and one poem in the *Kokinshū*.

Ki Wet-Nurse 紀乳母 (*Ki no menoto*, **dates unknown):** Ki no Zenshi (or Mataiko). She was married to one of Emperor Saga's sons and was Emperor Yōzei's wet-nurse. Her son Minamoto no Masaru was killed suddenly for no apparent reason in 883 by the fifteen-year old Emperor Yōzei, who appears to have suffered from mental illness and was forced to abdicate the following year. Author of two poems in the *Kokinshū*.

Kiyohara no Fukayabu 清原深養父 **(dates unknown):** A court official from the middle ranks of the aristocracy who was a contemporary of the *Kokinshū* compilers. Author of seventeen poems in the *Kokinshū*.

Kyōshin 敬信 **(dates unknown):** A nun who was Fujiwara no Yoruka's mother. Author of one poem in the *Kokinshū*.

Mibu no Tadamine 壬生忠岑 **(dates unknown):** A lower-ranking official who served as assistant to the Right Palace Guard. One of the four compilers of the *Kokinshū* and author of thirty-six poems.

Michinoku 陸奥 **(dates unknown):** Believed to be a daughter of Tachibana no Kuzunao 橘葛直, who was appointed governor of Iwami in 882. Author of one poem in the *Kokinshū*.

Miharu no Arisuke 御春有助 **(dates unknown):** A contemporary of the compilers. Author of two poems in the *Kokinshū*.

Minamoto no Masazumi 源当純 **(dates unknown):** Grandson of Emperor Montoku. Was appointed Minor Counselor in 903. Author of one poem in the *Kokinshū*.

Minamoto no Muneyuki 源宗于 **(d. 939):** Grandson of Emperor Kōkō and son of Prince Koretada. Author of six poems in the *Kokinshū*.

Minamoto no Tōru 源融 **(822–895):** A son of Emperor Saga, he was appointed Minister of the Left in 872 and held the position until his death. Referred to as the "Kawara Minister of the Left" in the *Kokinshū* and author of two poems.

Minamoto no Yoshiari 源能有 **(845–897):** Referred to in the *Kokinshū* as the "Imperial Kinsman Minister of the Right." A son of Emperor Montoku. Author of three poems in the *Kokinshū*.

Minister of the Left: *See* Fujiwara no Tokihira.

Mononobe no Yoshina 物部良名 **(dates unknown):** Nothing is known about this person, who is the author of one poem in the *Kokinshū*.

Muneoka no Ōyori 宗岡大頼 **(dates unknown):** Was a scholar of calculus and author of two poems in the *Kokinshū*.

Nijō Imperial Consort: *See* Fujiwara no Takaiko.

Ninna Emperor: *See* Emperor Kōkō.

Ōe no Chisato 大江千里 **(dates unknown):** A midranking aristocrat who was an older contemporary of the *Kokinshū* compilers. In 894, he submitted a poetry collection to the throne entitled *Kudai waka*, which is also known as "The Ōe no Chisato Collection." Author of ten poems in the *Kokinshū*.

Ono no Komachi 小野小町 **(dates unknown):** Active during the reigns of Ninmyō (833–850) and Montoku (850–858). One of the six poets from the recent past discussed in the Kana Preface and Mana Preface. Author of eighteen poems in the *Kokinshū*.

Ono no Sadaki 小野貞樹 **(dates unknown):** A midranking official who was appointed governor of Echigo in 860. Author of two poems in the *Kokinshū*.

Ono no Takamura no Ason 小野篁朝臣 **(802–852):** A scholar and poet, he served the courts of Saga, Junna, Ninmyō, and Montoku. He was a member of the embassy to the Tang court in 834, but remained behind because of a dispute, and was later exiled to Sanuki. He reached the third rank at the end of his career. Author of six poems in the *Kokinshū*.

Ono no Yoshiki 小野美材 **(d. 902):** A scholar of the classics, he served as an administrator in the province of Shinano. Author of two poems in the *Kokinshū*.

Ōshikōchi no Mitsune 凡河内躬恒 **(dates unknown):** One of the four compilers of the *Kokinshū*, he was appointed governor of Kai in 894. Author of 60 poems in the collection.

Ōtomo no Kuronushi 大伴黒主 **(dates unknown):** One of the six exemplary poets of the recent past mentioned in the Kana and Mana Prefaces. Author of three poems in the *Kokinshū*.

Sakai no Hitozane 酒井人真 **(d. 917):** Was governor of Tosa. Author of one poem in the *Kokinshū*.

Sakanoue no Korenori 坂上是則 **(dates unknown):** A contemporary of the *Kokinshū* compilers of a similar rank and professional career. Author of nine poems in the *Kokinshū*.

Shinsei 真静 **(dates unknown):** Practically nothing is known about this priest who is the author of two poems in the *Kokinshū*.

Sōku 承均 **(dates unknown):** A priest who was active during the late ninth century. Author of three poems in the *Kokinshū*.

Sosei 素性 **(dates unknown):** Henjō's son, he was active during Emperor Uda's reign. After entering the priesthood, he lived at the Urin Temple. Author of thirty-seven poems in the *Kokinshū*.

Sugano no Takayo 菅野高世 **(dates unknown):** He appears in historical records in the early ninth century. Was appointed governor of Suō Province in 820. Author of one poem in the *Kokinshū*.

Sugawara no Michizane 菅原道真 **(845–903):** Served Emperor Uda (866–931, r. 887–997) as Minister of the Right. Was a member of the embassy to the Tang Court in 894. In 901, he was exiled to Dazaifu, where he died two years later. Author of two poems in the *Kokinshū*.

Taira no Sadafumi 平貞文 **(d. 923):** A midranking official who sponsored a poetry contest in 905 and 906. Thought by some to be the basis for the hero of *The Tale of Heichū*. Author of nine poems in the *Kokinshū*.

Utsuku 寵 **(dates unknown):** A daughter of Minamoto no Kuwashi, who was appointed governor of Yamato in 895. Author of three poems in the *Kokinshū*.

Yūsen 幽仙 **(836–900):** A priest of the Fujiwara lineage. Author of two poems in the *Kokinshū*.

BIBLIOGRAPHY AND FURTHER READING

Abe Akio et al., eds. *Genji monogatari. Shinpen Nihon koten bungaku zenshū* 20-25. Tokyo: Shōgakkan, 1994.

Bodman, Richard W. *Poetics and Prosody in Early Mediaeval China: A Study and Translation of Kūkai's Bunkyō Hifuron*. Melbourne: Quirin Press, 2020. First published 1978.

Borgen, Robert. *Sugawara no Michizane and the Early Heian Court*. Honolulu: University of Hawai'i Press, 1996. First published 1984.

Brower, Robert H., and Earl Miner. *Japanese Court Poetry*. Stanford, CA: Stanford University Press, 1961.

Carter, Steven D. *How to Read a Japanese Poem*. New York: Columbia University Press, 2019.

——. "Waka in the Medieval Period: Patterns of Practice and Patronage." In *The Cambridge History of Japanese Literature*, ed. Haruo Shirane, Tomi Suzuki, and David Lurie, 238–255. Cambridge: Cambridge University Press, 2015.

Commons, Anne. "Japanese Poetic Thought, from Earliest Times to the Thirteenth Century." In *The Cambridge History of Japanese Literature*, ed. Haruo Shirane, Tomi Suzuki, and David Lurie, 218–229. Cambridge: Cambridge University Press, 2015.

Cook, Lewis Edwin. "The Discipline of Poetry: Authority and Invention in *The Kokindenju*." PhD diss., Cornell University, 2000.

——. "Waka and Commentary." In *Waka Opening Up to the World: Language, Community, and Gender*, ed. Haruo Shirane, 350–364. Tokyo: Bensei shuppan, 2012.

Cranston, Edwin. *A Waka Anthology.* Vol. 2, *Grasses of Remembrance.* Stanford, CA: Stanford University Press, 2006.

Denecke, Wiebke, Wai-Yee Li, and Xiaofei Tian. *The Oxford Handbook of Classical Chinese Literature (1000 BCE–900 CE).* New York: Oxford University Press, 2017.

Duthie, Torquil. *Man'yōshū and the Imperial Imagination in Early Japan.* Leiden: Brill, 2014.

——, ed. and trans. *Poesía Clásica Japonesa: Kokinwakashū.* Madrid: Editorial Trotta, 2005.

Egan, Ronald. "The Relationship of Calligraphy and Painting to Literature." In *The Oxford Handbook of Classical Chinese Literature (1000 BCE–900 CE),* ed. Wiebke Denecke, Wai-Yee Li, and Xiaofei Tian, 76–90. Oxford: Oxford University Press, 2017.

Felt, Mathieu. *Rewriting the Past: Textual Structure and Commentarial Legerdemain in Japan's First Official History.* PhD diss., Columbia University, 2017.

Fong, Wen C. "Chinese Calligraphy: Theory and History." In *The Embodied Image: Chinese Calligraphy from the John B. Elliott Collection,* ed. Robert E. Harrist, Jr. and Wen C. Fong, 29–84. Princeton, NJ: Princeton University Art Museum, 1999.

Fujioka Tadaharu, ed. *Fukurozōshi.* Vol. 1, *Shin Nihon koten bungaku taikei* 29. Tokyo: Iwanami shoten, 1995.

Fuller, Michael A. *An Introduction to Chinese Poetry: From the Canon of Poetry to the Lyrics of the Song Dynasty.* Cambridge, MA: Harvard University Asia Center, 2018.

Guest, Jennifer. *Primers, Commentaries, and Kanbun Literacy in Japanese Literary Culture (950–1250 CE).* PhD diss., Columbia University, 2013.

Harada Taneshige, and Takeda Akira, eds. *Monzen (Wen xuan): Bunshōhen. Shinshaku kanbun taikei* 82, 83, 93. Tokyo: Meiji shoin, 1994.

Harada Yoshioki. "Otokode, onnade meigi kō." In *Heian jidai bungaku goi kenkyū, zokuhen,* 1–11. Tokyo: Kazama shobō, 1973.

Hasegawa Masaharu et al., eds. *Tosa nikki, Kagerō nikki, Murasaki Shikibu nikki, Sarashina nikki. Shin Nihon koten bungaku taikei* 24. Tokyo: Iwanami shoten, 1989.

Heldt, Gustav. *The Pursuit of Harmony: Poetry and Power in Early Heian Japan.* Ithaca, NY: Cornell University Press, 2008.

Hirschfield, Jane. *The Ink Dark Moon: Love Poems by Ono no Komachi and Izumi Shikibu, Women of the Ancient Court of Japan.* New York: Vintage Books, 1990.

Huey, Robert N. "The Medievalization of Poetic Practice." *Harvard Journal of Asiatic Studies* 50, no. 2 (December 1990): 651–668.

Ishikawa Kyūyō. *Hiragana no bigaku.* Tokyo: Shinchōsha, 2007.

Ishikawa Tadahisa, ed. *Shikyō (Shijing). Shinshaku kanbun taikei* 110–112. Tokyo: Meiji shoin, 1997–2000.

Kamens, Edward. *Utamakura, Allusion, and Intertextuality in Traditional Japanese Poetry.* New Haven, CT: Yale University Press, 1997.

Katagiri Yōichi. *Kokinwakashū zenhyōshaku.* 3 vols. Tokyo: Kōdansha, 1998.

Kawai Kōzō et al., eds. *Monzen: Shihen 6.* Tokyo: Iwanami shoten, 2019.

Kern, Martin. "The Formation of the Classic of Poetry." In *The Homeric Epics and the Chinese Book of Songs: Foundational Texts Compared,* ed. Fritz-Heiner Mutschler, 39–71. Cambridge: Cambridge Scholars Publishing, 2018.

Kimbrough, R. Keller. "Reading the Miraculous Powers of Japanese Poetry: Spells, Truth Acts, and a Medieval Buddhist Poetics of the Supernatural." *Japanese Journal of Religious Studies* 32, no. 1 (2005): 1–33.

Klein, Susan Blakeley. *Allegories of Desire: Esoteric Literary Commentaries of Medieval Japan.* Cambridge, MA: Harvard University Asia Center, 2002.

——. *Dancing the Dharma: Religious and Political Allegory in Japanese Noh Theater.* Cambridge, MA: Harvard University Asia Center, 2021.

Kojima Noriyuki, and Arai Eizō, eds. *Kokinwakashū. Shin Nihon koten bungaku taikei* 5. Tokyo: Iwanami shoten, 1989.

Komatsu Hideo. *Kanabun no kōbun genri.* Augmented ed. Tokyo: Kasama shoin, 2003. First published 1997. New binding 2012.

——. *Koten waka kaidoku: Waka hyōgen wa dono yō ni shinka shita ka.* Tokyo: Kasama shoin, 2000.

——. *Miso hito moji no jojōshi: Kokinwakashū no waka hyōgen wo tokihogusu.* Tokyo: Kasama shoin, 2004.

——. *Nihongo shokishi genron.* Revised ed. Tokyo: Kasama shoin, 2000. First published 1998. New binding 2006.

——. *Teinei ni yomu koten.* Tokyo: Kasama shoin, 2008.

Kong Yingda. *Maoshi Zhengyi. Shisanjing zhushu* 4–6. Beijing: Beijing daxue chubanshe, 2000.

LaMarre, Thomas. *Uncovering Heian Japan: An Archaeology of Sensation and Inscription.* Durham, NC: Duke University Press, 2000.

Lurie, David B. *Realms of Literacy: Early Japan and the History of Writing.* Cambridge, MA: Harvard University Asia Center, 2011.

Masaoka Shiki. "Futatabi utayomi ni atauru sho." In *Shiki zenshū* 7, 23. Tokyo: Kōdansha, 1975.

——. "Jojibun." In *Shiki zenshū* 14, 241–49. Tokyo: Kōdansha, 1976.

McAuley, Thomas. *The Poetry Contest in Six Hundred Rounds: A Translation and Commentary.* 2 vols. Leiden: Brill, 2020.

McCullough, Helen. *Kokin Wakashu: The First Imperial Anthology of Japanese Poetry.* Stanford, CA: Stanford University Press, 1985.

Mori Hiromichi. *Nihon shoki no nazo o toku: Jussakusha wa dare ka.* Tokyo: Chūko Shinsho, 1999.

Nishiki Hitoshi. "Inseiki uta awase no kōzō to hōhō: 'Ke' kara 'hare' e no waka shikan no hihan." *Nihon bungaku* 43, no. 2 (1994): 24–33.

Nishimura Kayoko. "*Kokinshū* kanajo 'kochū' no seiritsu." *Chūko bungaku* 56 (1995): 10–18.

Nugent, Christopher M. B. "Literary Media: Writing and Orality." In *The Oxford Handbook of Classical Chinese Literature (1000 BCE–900 CE),* ed. Wiebke Denecke, Wai-Yee Li, and Xiaofei Tian, 46–60. Oxford: Oxford University Press, 2017.

Ogura Shigeji. "Kyūjū seiki no kana no shotai: Hiragana o chūshin to shite." *Kokuritsu rekishi minzoku hakubutsukan kenkyū hōkoku* 194 (March 2015): 171–185.

Ouyang Zhongshi, and Wen C. Fong. *Chinese Calligraphy.* Translated and edited by Wang Youfen. New Haven, CT: Yale University Press, 2008.

Owen, Stephen. "The Courtly Yongwu." Chapter 18 in *The Poetry of the Early Tang.* Melbourne: Quirin Press, 2012. First published 1977 by Yale University Press (New Haven, CT).

Persiani, Gian Piero. "The Public, the Private, and the In-Between: Poetry Exchanges as Court Diplomacy in Mid-Heian Japan." *Japan Review* 35 (2020): 7–29.

——. *Waka After the Kokinshū: Anatomy of a Cultural Phenomenon.* PhD diss., Columbia University, 2013.

Rabinovitch, Judith N., and Timothy R. Bradstock. *No Moonlight in My Cup: Sinitic Poetry (Kanshi) from the Japanese Court, Eighth to the Twelfth Centuries.* Leiden: Brill, 2019.

Richter, Antje. *Letters and Epistolary Culture in Early Medieval China.* Seattle: University of Washington Press, 2013.

Rodd, Laurel Rasplica. *Kokinshū: A Collection of Poems Ancient and Modern.* Princeton, NJ: Princeton University Press, 1984. Reprint, Cheng & Tsui Company, 1996.

Shibayama, Saeko. *Ōe no Masafusa and the Convergence of the "Ways": The Twilight of Early Chinese Literary Studies and the Rise of Waka Studies in the Long Twelfth Century in Japan*. PhD diss., Columbia University, 2012.

Shields, Anna M. *One Who Knows Me: Friendship and Literary Culture in Mid-Tang China*. Cambridge, MA: Harvard University Asia Center, 2015.

Shinada Yoshikazu. "*Man'yōshū*: The Invention of a National Poetry Anthology." In *Inventing the Classics: Modernity, National Identity, and Japanese Literature*, ed. Haruo Shirane and Tomi Suzuki, 31–50. Stanford, CA: Stanford University Press, 2002.

Shirane, Haruo, ed. *Traditional Japanese Literature: An Anthology, Beginnings to Sixteen Hundred*. New York: Columbia University Press, 2007.

Sorensen, Joseph T. *Optical Allusions: Screens, Paintings, and Poetry in Classical Japan (ca. 800–1200)*. Leiden: Brill, 2012.

Stavros, Matthew. *Kyoto: An Urban History of Japan's Premodern Capital*. Honolulu: University of Hawai'i Press, 2014.

Steininger, Brian. *Chinese Literary Forms in Heian Japan*. Cambridge, MA: Harvard University Asia Center, 2017.

——. "Li-Jiao's Songs: Commentary Based Reading and the Reception of Tang Poetry in Heian Japan." *East Asian Publishing and Society* 6, no. 2 (2016): 103–129.

Stilerman, Ariel. "Cultural Knowledge and Professional Training in the Poetic Treatises of Late Heian Japan." *Monumenta Nipponica* 72, no. 2 (2017): 153–187.

——. *Learning with Waka Poetry: Transmission and Production of Social Knowledge and Cultural Memory in Premodern Japan*. PhD diss., Columbia University, 2015.

Takeoka Masao. *Kokinwakashū zenhyōshaku*. 2 vols. Tokyo: Yūbun shōin, 1976.

Tian, Xiaofei. *Beacon Fire and Shooting Star: The Literary Culture of the Liang*. Cambridge, MA: Harvard Asia Center, 2007.

——. *The Halberd at Red Cliff: Jian'an and the Three Kingdoms*. Cambridge, MA: Harvard University Asia Center, 2018.

Uchida Sennosuke, and Ami Yūji, eds. *Monzen (Wen Xuan): Shihen. Shinshaku kanbun taikei* 14–16. Tokyo: Meiji shoin, 1963, 1964.

Unno Keisuke. "A History of Reading: Medieval Interpretations of the *Kokin wakashū*." In *Waka Opening up to the World: Language, Community, and Gender*, ed. Haruo Shirane, 340–349. Tokyo: Bensei shuppan, 2012.

Van Goethem, Ellen. *Nagaoka: Japan's Forgotten Capital.* Leiden: Brill, 2008.

Watanabe Yasuaki. *Waka to wa nanika.* Tokyo: Iwanami shinsho, 2009.

Wixted, Timothy. "The *Kokinshū* Prefaces: Another Perspective." *Harvard Journal of Asiatic Studies* 43, no. 1 (June 1983): 215–238.

Yoda, Tomiko. *Gender and National Literature: Heian Texts in the Constructions of Japanese Modernity.* Durham, NC: Duke University Press, 2004.

INDEX

Classics, 240, 242
classified encyclopedias *(leishu)*, 284
"close to the ears of the people,"
13, 13n20
clouds, 29, 58, 81, 95, 102, 119; age
related to, 101; blossoms related
to, 94; heaven related to, 226,
226n4, 283; in Love Songs 2,
137; in Love Songs 5, 171; in
Miscellaneous Songs 1, 189
clover, 70, 71, 229
cockerel, 146, 149
collection *(shū)*, 1
*Collection for One Thousand Years
(Senzaishū)*, 341–42
*Collection of Ancient and Modern
Japanese Songs.* See *Kokinshū*
*Collection of Japanese and Chinese
Compositions for Chanting
(Wakan rōeishū)*, 330
*Collection of Later Gleanings
(Goshūishū)*, 340–41
*Collection of Later Selections of Japanese
Poetry (Gosenwakashū)*, 339–40
Collection of Myriad Ages. See
Man'yōshū
colors, 30–31, 32, 40, 45–46, 79,
79n24; of cherry blossoms,
364; fading of, 182, 360–61; of
garments, 75, 85; of hearts, 47,
365; of leaves, 68, 80, 82–85,
86, 87, 89, 170, 174, 223; in
Miscellaneous Songs 1, 194;
of plum blossoms, 97. *See also
specific colors*
Conception and Structure of
Kokinshū. See *Kokinshū*
conception and structure

Confucius, 240, 322, 336n3; *Analects*
of, 242, 244, 331–32, 338n27
confusion, 41, 66, 117, 121, 150
Cook, Lewis, 347–48, 368n12
cranes, 192, 192nn44–45, 218
Cranston, Edwin (EC), 359, 360, 361,
363, 367n5
crickets, 64, 124
criticism, 12, 14, 14n25, 324–26,
337nn19–20
crown prince (Spring Prince), 22,
22n4, 102, 102n31
crying, 160, 168. *See also* tears
cuckoo, 54, 55, 57, 114, 120, 149, 182
cursive *kana*, 306; in Heian Court
and Kana Writing, 255, 259, 261,
262–63, 267n10, 267n18

dai. See topics
Daigo (Emperor), 221, 221n53, 271;
Kana Preface and, 233–34, 233n19,
328, 329; Kana Preface and Mana
Preface on, 322–23; in *Kokinshū*
Prefaces, 322–23; poems by, 26,
26n7, 28, 28n8
dai shirazu. See topics unknown
darkness, 32, 129, 150
Date Masamune, 351n12
dawn, 57, 58, 62, 63, 95, 109, 124; in
Love Songs 3, 146, 148, 149; in
Love Songs 4, 157; in Love Songs
5, 167, 168
death, 215; Ise on, 276; longing related
to, 134; loving related to, 157; of
Saichō, 261–62; of Tameie, 345
deer, 69, 70, 89
dew, 71n20; in autumn, 79,
79n24; beads of, 28; from

5/7/5/7/7 syllabic pattern, 247–49,
251, 254n11, 301, 302; English
translation of, 357–59, 367n5
flight, 43, 106, 132
flowers, 49, 101, 211, 308; on
branches, 227; maiden, 72–74,
327; moon, 75
forgetting, 135, 159, 165, 169
formal *(hare)*, 288–89
formal/ordinary *(hare/ke)*, 288–90
forthright song, 229
fragrance. *See* scent
frog, 50, 225
frost, 71, 86, 132, 133, 201, 228
Fuji River, 220
Fujiwara Kachion, 203
Fujiwara Kunitsune no Ason, 148
Fujiwara Michimune, 344
Fujiwara no Hamanari, 309n1
Fujiwara no Kachion, 115
Fujiwara no Kanesuke, 210
Fujiwara no Kintō, 330
Fujiwara no Kiyō, 104, 104nn32–33
Fujiwara no Kiyosuke, 328–29
Fujiwara no Koremoto, 183
Fujiwara no Koreoka, 105
Fujiwara no Kotonao, 23
Fujiwara no Morotada, 350n2
Fujiwara no Mototoshi, 344
Fujiwara no Mototsune, 20n2,
101, 101n29
Fujiwara no Norinaga, 351n11
Fujiwara no Okikaze: in Love Songs
2, 134; in Spring Songs 2, 45–46
Fujiwara no Onshi, 37, 37n11
Fujiwara no Sekio, 86
Fujiwara no Sugane no Ason, 68
Fujiwara no Sukeyo, 337n18

Fujiwara no Tadafusa: in Autumn
Songs 1, 66, 66n19; in
Miscellaneous Songs 2, 201
Fujiwara no Tadayuki, 154
Fujiwara no Takaiko, 20, 20n2
Fujiwara no Teika, 338n23, 341–42; in
Kokinshū text and commentarial
tradition, 344–45, 351n12; in
Kokinshū translation, 353–54,
356–57, 366n3
Fujiwara no Tokihira (Minister of
the Left), 74, 74n22
Fujiwara no Toshiyuki Ason, 131,
281n10, 295–97; in Autumn Songs
1, 60; in Autumn Songs 2, 79,
79n24, 81; in Love Songs 3, 142,
148; in Love Songs 4, 158; in
Songs of the East, 223
Fujiwara no Yoruka, 102, 102n31, 160,
295–96
Fujiwara no Yoshifusa, 21, 21n3, 35,
35n9, 273
Fujiwara Sadazane, 351n10
Fujiwara Takatsune no Ason, 182
Fukayabu, 58
Fukiage Beach, 81
Fukurozōshi (Fujiwara no Kiyosuke),
328–29
Fuller, Michael, 336n7
"full-form" sinographs. See *mana*
Funya no Asayasu, 72
Funya no Yasuhide (Fun'ya no
Yasuhide) (Bunrin), 11n16, 22, 78,
232, 232n17, 298, 325, 337n20
Furu no Imamichi, 73, 73n21

Gangyō accession, 220, 220n51
Gangyōji temple, 49, 49n15

puns *(kakekotoba)*, 48, 48n14, 98,
98n27, 276; in Farewell Songs,
104, 104nn34–35; in Kana Preface,
225, 225n2, 228, 228n10, 333–34,
338n30; in *Kokinshū* translation,
361; in Literary Sinitic, 264,
268n21; in Love Songs 1, 114,
114n37; in Prosody and Rhetorical
Conventions, 306–8; in Travel
Songs, 110, 110n36

questions, 23, 156, 209, 361

rain, 83, 87, 92, 117, 148, 158; in Love
Songs 5, 174; in Spring Songs 2,
44, 48, 48n14, 51
"reading by gloss" *(kundoku)*, 244–45,
253n5, 332–33
reality, 151, 198; dreams or, 149, 150, 303
Record of Rites, 7n1
Records of Ancient Matters. See *Kojiki*
reflection, 154, 160, 221, 230, 361–62
regrets, 40, 105, 123, 149, 172, 214
responses, 117, 170, 254n14, 267n16,
290; to cries, 122; by Komachi,
130; by Minamoto no Yoshiari,
161, 161n40; by Muneoka no
Ōyori, 200; by Narihira no Ason,
143, 150, 171
"rhapsodies" *(shifu)*, 242–43
Rhythmes Japonais (Bonneau), 367n7
rivers, 123, 133, 203; Asuka, 83,
98, 98n27, 196, 235; Fuji, 220;
heavenly, 61–62, 61n16, 63, 186,
210; Hinokuma, 219; Mitarashi,
121; Ōi, 192, 192nn44–45, 291;
"Spring," 292; Sumida, 111;
Tatsuta, 83, 88, 92, 145, 231, 291–92;

of tears, 142, 143; Tomi, 9, 9n8;
Yoshino, 115, 177, 230, 305
rocks, 100, 115, 155, 305; criticism
related to, 14, 14n25
Rodd, Laurel (LR), 338n25, 359, 360,
361, 363, 367n5
Rokujō House, 341–42
royal songs from great bureau, 218,
218n48
Ryōdō no kikigaki (Two Readings)
(Sōgi), 361

Sadatoki (Prince), 104, 104n32
sadness, 64–65, 69, 84, 139, 147;
in Love Songs 5, 174–76; in
Miscellaneous Songs 1, 193
Saga (Emperor), 261–62, 269
Saichō, 261–62
Sakanoue no Korenori, 95, 176
sand, 100, 221, 228
Sanjō no Machi, 194
Sanskrit, 247
Sarumaru no Daifu, 12, 12n18
scarlet leaves, 62, 69, 80, 207, 231, 293; in
Autumn Songs 2, 82–85, 86, 87, 89
scattered blossoms, 40–41, 42, 43, 44,
48, 50
scents, 45–46, 55, 97; in Spring Songs
1, 30–31, 32, 33
sea, 78, 100, 202, 322
Sea Deity, 8, 8n5, 262–63
seasonal order, 281n13, 286–87, 292
seasonal poems, 234, 234n21, 277, 298.
See also specific seasons
secret, 133
Secret Archive of the Mirror of Letters,
The (Bunkyōhifuron) (Wang
Changling), 337n19

TRANSLATIONS FROM THE
ASIAN CLASSICS

Major Plays of Chikamatsu, tr. Donald Keene 1961

Four Major Plays of Chikamatsu, tr. Donald Keene. Paperback ed. only. 1961; rev. ed. 1997

Records of the Grand Historian of China, translated from the Shih chi of Ssu-ma Ch'ien, tr. Burton Watson, 2 vols. 1961

Instructions for Practical Living and Other Neo-Confucian Writings by Wang Yang-ming, tr. Wing-tsit Chan 1963

Hsün Tzu: Basic Writings, tr. Burton Watson, paperback ed. only. 1963; rev. ed. 1996

Chuang Tzu: Basic Writings, tr. Burton Watson, paperback ed. only. 1964; rev. ed. 1996

The Mahābhārata, tr. Chakravarthi V. Narasimhan. Also in paperback ed. 1965; rev. ed. 1997

The Manyōshū, Nippon Gakujutsu Shinkōkai edition 1965

Su Tung-p'o: Selections from a Sung Dynasty Poet, tr. Burton Watson. Also in paperback ed. 1965

Bhartrihari: Poems, tr. Barbara Stoler Miller. Also in paperback ed. 1967

Basic Writings of Mo Tzu, Hsün Tzu, and Han Fei Tzu, tr. Burton Watson. Also in separate paperback eds. 1967

The Awakening of Faith, Attributed to Aśvaghosha, tr. Yoshito S. Hakeda. Also in paperback ed. 1967

Reflections on Things at Hand: The Neo-Confucian Anthology, comp. Chu Hsi and Lü Tsu-ch'ien, tr. Wing-tsit Chan 1967

The Platform Sutra of the Sixth Patriarch, tr. Philip B. Yampolsky. Also in paperback ed. 1967

Essays in Idleness: The Tsurezuregusa of Kenkō, tr. Donald Keene. Also in paperback ed. 1967

The Pillow Book of Sei Shōnagon, tr. Ivan Morris, 2 vols. 1967

Two Plays of Ancient India: The Little Clay Cart and the Minister's Seal, tr. J. A. B. van Buitenen 1968

The Complete Works of Chuang Tzu, tr. Burton Watson 1968

The Romance of the Western Chamber (Hsi Hsiang Chi), tr. S. I. Hsiung. Also in paperback ed. 1968

The Manyōshū, Nippon Gakujutsu Shinkōkai edition. Paperback ed. only. 1969

Records of the Historian: Chapters from the Shih chi of Ssu-ma Ch'ien, tr. Burton Watson. Paperback ed. only. 1969

Cold Mountain: 100 Poems by the T'ang Poet Han-shan, tr. Burton Watson. Also in paperback ed. 1970

Twenty Plays of the Nō Theatre, ed. Donald Keene. Also in paperback ed. 1970

Chūshingura: The Treasury of Loyal Retainers, tr. Donald Keene. Also in paperback ed. 1971; rev. ed. 1997

The Zen Master Hakuin: Selected Writings, tr. Philip B. Yampolsky 1971

Chinese Rhyme-Prose: Poems in the Fu Form from the Han and Six Dynasties Periods, tr. Burton Watson. Also in paperback ed. 1971

Kūkai: Major Works, tr. Yoshito S. Hakeda. Also in paperback ed. 1972

The Old Man Who Does as He Pleases: Selections from the Poetry and Prose of Lu Yu, tr. Burton Watson 1973

The Lion's Roar of Queen Śrīmālā, tr. Alex and Hideko Wayman 1974

Courtier and Commoner in Ancient China: Selections from the History of the Former Han by Pan Ku, tr. Burton Watson. Also in paperback ed. 1974

Japanese Literature in Chinese, vol. 1: *Poetry and Prose in Chinese by Japanese Writers of the Early Period,* tr. Burton Watson 1975

Japanese Literature in Chinese, vol. 2: *Poetry and Prose in Chinese by Japanese Writers of the Later Period,* tr. Burton Watson 1976

Love Song of the Dark Lord: Jayadeva's Gītagovinda, tr. Barbara Stoler Miller. Also in paperback ed. Cloth ed. includes critical text of the Sanskrit. 1977; rev. ed. 1997

Ryōkan: Zen Monk-Poet of Japan, tr. Burton Watson 1977

Calming the Mind and Discerning the Real: From the Lam rim chen mo of Tson-kha-pa, tr. Alex Wayman 1978

The Hermit and the Love-Thief: Sanskrit Poems of Bhartrihari and Bilhaṇa, tr. Barbara Stoler Miller 1978

The Lute: Kao Ming's P'i-p'a chi, tr. Jean Mulligan. Also in paperback ed. 1980

A Chronicle of Gods and Sovereigns: Jinnō Shōtōki of Kitabatake Chikafusa, tr. H. Paul Varley 1980

Among the Flowers: The Hua-chien chi, tr. Lois Fusek 1982

Grass Hill: Poems and Prose by the Japanese Monk Gensei, tr. Burton Watson 1983

Doctors, Diviners, and Magicians of Ancient China: Biographies of Fang-shih, tr. Kenneth J. DeWoskin. Also in paperback ed. 1983

Theater of Memory: The Plays of Kālidāsa, ed. Barbara Stoler Miller. Also in paperback ed. 1984

The Columbia Book of Chinese Poetry: From Early Times to the Thirteenth Century, ed. and tr. Burton Watson. Also in paperback ed. 1984

Poems of Love and War: From the Eight Anthologies and the Ten Long Poems of Classical Tamil, tr. A. K. Ramanujan. Also in paperback ed. 1985

The Bhagavad Gita: Krishna's Counsel in Time of War, tr. Barbara Stoler Miller 1986

The Columbia Book of Later Chinese Poetry, ed. and tr. Jonathan Chaves. Also in paperback ed. 1986

The Tso Chuan: Selections from China's Oldest Narrative History, tr. Burton Watson 1989

Waiting for the Wind: Thirty-Six Poets of Japan's Late Medieval Age, tr. Steven Carter 1989

Selected Writings of Nichiren, ed. Philip B. Yampolsky 1990

Saigyō, Poems of a Mountain Home, tr. Burton Watson 1990

The Book of Lieh Tzu: A Classic of the Tao, tr. A. C. Graham. Morningside ed. 1990

The Tale of an Anklet: An Epic of South India—The Cilappatikāram of Iḷaṅko Aṭikaḷ, tr. R. Parthasarathy 1993

Waiting for the Dawn: A Plan for the Prince, tr. with introduction by Wm. Theodore de Bary 1993

Yoshitsune and the Thousand Cherry Trees: A Masterpiece of the Eighteenth-Century Japanese Puppet Theater, tr., annotated, and with introduction by Stanleigh H. Jones Jr. 1993

The Lotus Sutra, tr. Burton Watson. Also in paperback ed. 1993

The Classic of Changes: A New Translation of the I Ching as Interpreted by Wang Bi, tr. Richard John Lynn 1994

Beyond Spring: Tz'u Poems of the Sung Dynasty, tr. Julie Landau 1994

The Columbia Anthology of Traditional Chinese Literature, ed. Victor H. Mair 1994

Scenes for Mandarins: The Elite Theater of the Ming, tr. Cyril Birch 1995

Letters of Nichiren, ed. Philip B. Yampolsky; tr. Burton Watson et al. 1996

Unforgotten Dreams: Poems by the Zen Monk Shōtetsu, tr. Steven D. Carter 1997

The Vimalakirti Sutra, tr. Burton Watson 1997

Japanese and Chinese Poems to Sing: The Wakan rōei shū, tr. J. Thomas Rimer and Jonathan Chaves 1997

Breeze Through Bamboo: Kanshi of Ema Saikō, tr. Hiroaki Sato 1998

A Tower for the Summer Heat, by Li Yu, tr. Patrick Hanan 1998

Traditional Japanese Theater: An Anthology of Plays, by Karen Brazell 1998

The Original Analects: Sayings of Confucius and His Successors (0479–0249), by E. Bruce Brooks and A. Taeko Brooks 1998

The Classic of the Way and Virtue: A New Translation of the Tao-te ching of Laozi as Interpreted by Wang Bi, tr. Richard John Lynn 1999

The Four Hundred Songs of War and Wisdom: An Anthology of Poems from Classical Tamil, The Puranāṇūru, ed. and tr. George L. Hart and Hank Heifetz 1999

Original Tao: Inward Training (Nei-yeh) *and the Foundations of Taoist Mysticism*, by Harold D. Roth 1999

Po Chü-i: Selected Poems, tr. Burton Watson 2000

Lao Tzu's Tao Te Ching: *A Translation of the Startling New Documents Found at Guodian*, by Robert G. Henricks 2000

The Shorter Columbia Anthology of Traditional Chinese Literature, ed. Victor H. Mair 2000

Mistress and Maid (Jiaohongji), by Meng Chengshun, tr. Cyril Birch 2001

Chikamatsu: Five Late Plays, tr. and ed. C. Andrew Gerstle 2001

The Essential Lotus: Selections from the Lotus Sutra, tr. Burton Watson 2002

Early Modern Japanese Literature: An Anthology, 1600–1900, ed. Haruo Shirane 2002; abridged 2008

The Columbia Anthology of Traditional Korean Poetry, ed. Peter H. Lee 2002

The Sound of the Kiss, or The Story That Must Never Be Told: Pingali Suranna's Kalapurnodayamu, tr. Vecheru Narayana Rao and David Shulman 2003

The Selected Poems of Du Fu, tr. Burton Watson 2003

Far Beyond the Field: Haiku by Japanese Women, tr. Makoto Ueda 2003

Just Living: Poems and Prose by the Japanese Monk Tonna, ed. and tr. Steven D. Carter 2003

Han Feizi: Basic Writings, tr. Burton Watson 2003

Mozi: Basic Writings, tr. Burton Watson 2003

Xunzi: Basic Writings, tr. Burton Watson 2003

Zhuangzi: Basic Writings, tr. Burton Watson 2003

The Awakening of Faith, Attributed to Aśvaghosha, tr. Yoshito S. Hakeda, introduction by Ryūichi Abé 2005

The Tales of the Heike, tr. Burton Watson, ed. Haruo Shirane 2006

Tales of Moonlight and Rain, by Ueda Akinari, tr. with introduction by Anthony H. Chambers 2007

Traditional Japanese Literature: An Anthology, Beginnings to 1600, ed. Haruo Shirane 2007

The Philosophy of Qi, by Kaibara Ekken, tr. Mary Evelyn Tucker 2007

The Analects of Confucius, tr. Burton Watson 2007

The Art of War: Sun Zi's Military Methods, tr. Victor Mair 2007

One Hundred Poets, One Poem Each: A Translation of the Ogura Hyakunin Isshu, tr. Peter McMillan 2008

Zeami: Performance Notes, tr. Tom Hare 2008

Zongmi on Chan, tr. Jeffrey Lyle Broughton 2009

Scripture of the Lotus Blossom of the Fine Dharma, rev. ed., tr. Leon Hurvitz, preface and introduction by Stephen R. Teiser 2009

Mencius, tr. Irene Bloom, ed. with an introduction by Philip J. Ivanhoe 2009

Clouds Thick, Whereabouts Unknown: Poems by Zen Monks of China, tr. Charles Egan 2010

The Mozi: A Complete Translation, tr. Ian Johnston 2010

The Huainanzi: A Guide to the Theory and Practice of Government in Early Han China, by Liu An, tr. and ed. John S. Major, Sarah A. Queen, Andrew Seth Meyer, and Harold D. Roth, with Michael Puett and Judson Murray 2010

The Demon at Agi Bridge and Other Japanese Tales, tr. Burton Watson, ed. with introduction by Haruo Shirane 2011

Haiku Before Haiku: From the Renga Masters to Bashō, tr. with introduction by Steven D. Carter 2011

The Columbia Anthology of Chinese Folk and Popular Literature, ed. Victor H. Mair and Mark Bender 2011

Tamil Love Poetry: The Five Hundred Short Poems of the Aiṅkuṟunūṟu, tr. and ed. Martha Ann Selby 2011

The Teachings of Master Wuzhu: Zen and Religion of No-Religion, by Wendi L. Adamek 2011

The Essential Huainanzi, by Liu An, tr. and ed. John S. Major, Sarah A. Queen, Andrew Seth Meyer, and Harold D. Roth 2012

The Dao of the Military: Liu An's Art of War, tr. Andrew Seth Meyer 2012

Unearthing the Changes: Recently Discovered Manuscripts of the Yi

Jing (I Ching) *and Related Texts*, by
    Edward L. Shaughnessy 2013
*Record of Miraculous Events in Japan:
    The* Nihon ryōiki, tr. Burton
    Watson 2013
The Complete Works of Zhuangzi, tr.
    Burton Watson 2013
Lust, Commerce, and Corruption: An
    Account of What I Have Seen
    and Heard, *by an Edo Samurai*, tr.
    and ed. Mark Teeuwen and Kate
    Wildman Nakai with Miyazaki
    Fumiko, Anne Walthall, and John
    Breen 2014; abridged 2017
Exemplary Women of Early China: The
    Lienü zhuan *of Liu Xiang*, tr. Anne
    Behnke Kinney 2014
The Columbia Anthology of Yuan Drama,
    ed. C. T. Hsia, Wai-yee Li, and
    George Kao 2014
*The Resurrected Skeleton: From Zhuangzi
    to Lu Xun*, by Wilt L. Idema 2014
The Sarashina Diary: *A Woman's Life
    in Eleventh-Century Japan*, by
    Sugawara no Takasue no Musume,
    tr. with introduction by Sonja
    Arntzen and Itō Moriyuki 2014;
    reader's edition 2018
The Kojiki: *An Account of Ancient
    Matters*, by Ō no Yasumaro, tr.
    Gustav Heldt 2014
The Orphan of Zhao *and Other Yuan
    Plays: The Earliest Known Versions*,
    tr. and introduced by Stephen H.
    West and Wilt L. Idema 2014
Luxuriant Gems of the Spring and
    Autumn, attributed to Dong
    Zhongshu, ed. and tr. Sarah A.
    Queen and John S. Major 2016
*A Book to Burn and a Book to Keep
    (Hidden): Selected Writings*, by Li

Zhi, ed. and tr. Rivi Handler-Spitz,
    Pauline Lee, and Haun Saussy 2016
The Shenzi Fragments: *A Philosophical
    Analysis and Translation*, by Eirik
    Lang Harris 2016
Record of Daily Knowledge *and* Poems
    and Essays: *Selections*, by Gu Yanwu,
    tr. and ed. Ian Johnston 2017
*The Book of Lord Shang: Apologetics
    of State Power in Early China*, by
    Shang Yang, ed. and tr. Yuri Pines
    2017; abridged edition 2019
*The Songs of Chu: An Ancient Anthology
    of Works by Qu Yuan and Others*, ed.
    and tr. Gopal Sukhu 2017
Ghalib: Selected Poems and Letters, by
    Mirza Asadullah Khan Ghalib, tr.
    Frances W. Pritchett and Owen T.
    A. Cornwall 2017
*Quelling the Demons' Revolt: A Novel
    from Ming China*, attributed to Luo
    Guanzhong, tr. Patrick Hanan 2017
*Erotic Poems from the Sanskrit:
    A New Translation*, ed. and tr.
    R. Parthasarathy 2017
*The Book of Swindles: Selections from
    a Late Ming Collection*, by Zhang
    Yingyu, tr. Christopher G. Rea and
    Bruce Rusk 2017
*Monsters, Animals, and Other Worlds: A
    Collection of Short Medieval Japanese
    Tales*, ed. R. Keller Kimbrough and
    Haruo Shirane 2018
*Hidden and Visible Realms: Early Medieval
    Chinese Tales of the Supernatural and
    the Fantastic*, compiled by Liu Yiqing,
    ed. and tr. Zhenjun Zhang 2018
*A Couple of Soles: A Comic Play from
    Seventeenth-Century China*, by
    Li Yu, tr. Jing Shen and Robert E.
    Hegel 2019

The Original Meaning of the Yijing: *Commentary on the* Scripture of Change, by Zhu Xi, tr. and ed. Joseph A. Adler 2019

Plum Shadows and Plank Bridge: Two Memoirs About Courtesans, by Mao Xiang and Yu Huai, tr. and ed. Wai-yee Li 2020

The Diary of 1636: The Second Manchu Invasion of Korea, by Na Man'gap, tr. with introduction by George Kallander 2020

Top Graduate Zhang Xie: The Earliest Extant Chinese Southern Play, tr. and introduced by Regina S. Llamas 2020

In the Shelter of the Pine: A Memoir of Yanagisawa Yoshiyasu and Tokugawa Japan, by Ōgimachi Machiko, tr. G. G. Rowley 2021

Zhuangzi: A New Translation of the Sayings of Master Zhuang as Interpreted by Guo Xiang, tr. Richard John Lynn 2022

The Fragrant Companions: A Play About Love Between Women, by Li Yu, tr. Stephen Roddy and Ying Wang 2022

GPSR Authorized Representative: Easy Access System Europe, Mustamäe tee 50, 10621 Tallinn, Estonia, gpsr.requests@easproject.com